AMAZING MAISY

KAY LEWIS

For my daughter Maisy, this book is dedicated to you.
You can now finally read about the journey you went through at
such a young age
and all the love and support you had along the way.
You are very brave and I am so proud of you, love you Maisy
Moo x

1

WHERE IT BEGINS

2004

*M*aisy was a happy and gorgeous, nine-and-a-half-month-old baby who always had a big smile on her face. We were always together. I never wanted to leave her, and quite simply, I adored her.

She had small features and was such a good baby. I'd hoped for a girl as my first child and couldn't wait to go shopping and buy pretty girlie clothes.

A few weeks before my due date, February 14th, 2004, I started getting pains in my side. I was sitting at my work desk trying to ignore the pain, but it just continued to get worse. I phoned my mum for advice. She had four children, so she was always good to talk to for baby advice.

I explained that I'd woken up in pain that morning, and Mum suggested that it could be the baby lying on a nerve and that hopefully, once the baby moved, it would ease.

I carried on working, but by lunchtime I was struggling to even walk. My boss told me to go straight to the hospital. I drove myself to Harold Wood hospital and waited at the maternity clinic to be seen. The nurse checked my temperature, felt the baby, and told me I had a water infection, for which I was given antibiotics and advised to go home and rest. She assured me I'd feel better in a couple of days.

However, after a few days resting on the sofa at home, I still wasn't feeling much better, but I was due a home visit from the midwife the following day so I didn't call the doctor. When the midwife came, she told me I needed to return to hospital. This wasn't a water infection, she said, as the pain was too strong, and the medication hadn't improved the symptoms.

On the way back to Harold Wood hospital I picked up my best friend Toni for a bit of support.

We sat waiting at the maternity clinic until finally my name was called. The doctor asked me a few questions, felt my stomach, and advised that he wanted to do a scan on the area. A nurse came to take me down for a scan while Toni was shown to a cubicle to wait for my return. I wasn't gone long, and returned to the cubicle where Toni and I sat chatting while we waited for the results.

After 20 minutes or so the doctor returned, sat down, and explained that I had only one working kidney! He said my left kidney is the size of a peanut and only works at 13 per cent, while my right kidney is double the size of a normal kidney and working at 87 per cent, doing twice the work.

I was 25 years old and never knew this! As you can imagine, I was in complete shock. The doctor went on to explain that the baby was lying on the enlarged kidney, which was why I was in severe pain.

Due to the baby causing me this much discomfort, they advised that they needed to get the baby out as soon as possible, or it could cause further damage to my good kidney. Toni and I looked at each other, I think we must have been in shock as we even laughed.

I left the hospital stunned and immediately phoned my

mum to tell her what the doctor had said. Naturally, she was completely shocked too. and straight away offered me her kidney if I needed a kidney transplant! I told her the doctor didn't seem to think this was necessary, and that he was more concerned about getting the baby out quickly. After the baby was born they would check my kidney function.

I called Sam, my husband, to tell him about my kidneys and that I was waiting for an appointment to be induced, which could be in the next few days. We were all shell-shocked, especially my mum. She kept phoning me all day, still insisting I have her kidney!

MAISY'S BIRTH

31ST JANUARY 2004

*S*am and my mum were my birthing partners and sat with me while I was waiting to be induced. The room was very relaxed, with soft music playing, and I was very calm considering it was my first birth and I'd been watching lots of birthing programmes over the last few days. I couldn't wait to meet her. I was induced later that morning and Maisy was born weighing 7lbs 7oz at 5.51pm after seven-and-a-half hours of labour under the care of Dr Marilyn Smith and midwife, Debbie Newell.

She was absolutely gorgeous - 52 centimetres long and with tiny features and beautiful, big blue eyes. We named her Maisy Rose Bradford; a name Sam had found in a baby name book.

Even though it was quite late that night, the hospital allowed my dad and Sam's parents to meet their first grandchild and we took some lovely photos of them all holding our beautiful Maisy.

After Maisy was checked over by the nurse the next day, we were discharged later that afternoon.

Being home was lovely. I was getting myself into a

routine with Maisy and she was so good, although I was having trouble breast feeding. It was unbearably painful and after five days I had to stop. I was really gutted as I wanted to continue but I could no longer bear the agony every time she latched on to feed.

Wherever I went Maisy went with me. I had a baby carrier that she would happily go in whilst we walked our puppy, Lola. Lola loved Maisy, and when Maisy slept in her Moses basket in the living room, you would always find Lola lying next to her.

We were always out visiting friends and family and going for long walks, plus the odd shopping trip to Romford Mothercare. We had a lovely cottage in Rainham, Essex, that Sam had been decorating and our families were all close by. Life was good. But when Maisy was around two months old, we decided to sell our house and move to Tenerife, where we have family.

We soon settled into Tenerife life. Sam got a job working in a bar in a resort called Island Village, and I cleaned my sister's house twice a week. We lived in an apartment in Torviscas Alto in Adeje and we were all happy.

One day I went shopping with my sister, Paula, in Los Cristianos, pushing Maisy in her pram. We bumped into Rita, a doctor friend of Paula's, and chatted for a while. Later that evening Paula received a text from Rita to say she recommended that I took Maisy to have her eyes checked. We weren't concerned as we hadn't noticed any problems with her eyes. Paula got in touch with her doctor, and we were waiting to hear back with an appointment for Maisy. But we never ended up attending.

THE FIRST SIGNS

21ST NOVEMBER 2004

*M*aisy had woken up her usual happy self that morning, but she had a red mark under her left eye and her right eye looked glossy. I assumed she might have something in it, but after breakfast I noticed her eye still looked sore. It didn't seem to be bothering Maisy, but by lunchtime her left eye started to look bigger than her right eye, like it was being pushed out of its socket. Sam and I agreed we needed to take her to the hospital. I phoned my sister, Paula, and asked her to come with me as she spoke Spanish and we needed someone to translate. A rep that worked on Paula's resort managed to get us an appointment at San Eugenio Clinic to see a specialist and that evening me, Sam and Paula waited outside the emergency entrance at San Eugenio Clinic near to where we lived.

After waiting for a while, Maisy's name was called, and we followed a doctor to a corridor where he examined Maisy in her push chair. The doctor looked at her eyes and told us that he thought Maisy was blind in both eyes. I knew something was wrong but didn't agree that she was blind. The doctor told us that we needed to take Maisy to a hospital in the north of the island as they had more equipment and specialist doctors. He told us which doctor we needed to see and at what time we should be there. I remember us being there really early the next morning.

> **Memory from Paula:** *I remember being with Kay at the clinic and the doctor was very concerned and said that we needed to go to the hospital urgently. I can't remember the doctor's name, but he was really kind and thorough.*

The next morning, Sam, Paula, Maisy and I drove to the emergency clinic at the Universitario Hospital in the north. The doctor tried to shine a torch into Maisy's eyes while she sat in my arms but Maisy was not happy and she wouldn't sit or lay still for the doctors to have a good look at her eyes. The doctors said it may be glaucoma, but they continued to try and do further checks before giving up and deciding that she'd have to try again the following day with Maisy under anaesthetic.

Paula was unable to come with us that next day as she was working and then flying to London that evening with friends for a holiday. Carlos, who worked with my sister, came with us to help translate instead. After waiting ages, a doctor took Maisy from my arms and said that he'd be about 20 minutes.

In the waiting area the three of us waited anxiously and hardly spoke. I was constantly looking at my watch to check the time. Twenty minutes went by. I stared at the door where Maisy had entered. I felt sick with worry as another ten minutes passed. The more time we were left waiting, the more I kept thinking the worst.

It had now been 40 minutes and I had a bad feeling and wanted to cry. Carlos could see I was anxious and went to speak to one of the receptionists. He called me over and pointed towards a door.

I went in and could hear Maisy screaming. She was in a cot sobbing so I picked her up to calm her. She was so upset and sleepy from the anaesthetic. Sam appeared by my side within minutes and suggested we go back to England and visit Moorfields Eye Hospital where there was an eye specialist. He knew there was something seriously wrong. He showed me a small photo he'd just been given by a doctor. It was a scan showing white dots in and around both of Maisy's eyes.

The three of us drove back home in silence. I didn't want to speak, I couldn't. I was so confused by what the doctors had said and knew we had to go back to London. I remember thinking this must be serious if the doctors here in Tenerife weren't even sure what the white dots were. Sam called my sister, and brother-in-law, Tom, who managed to get us flights to the UK that night. Someone Tom knew had given up their flights up for us. (I recently asked Tom if he remembered any details of who they were, but he just said at 58 he struggles to remember what happened last week, let alone two decades ago!).

Memory from Tina: *I think it was Paula that phoned me to say what had happened at the hospital with Maisy. Paula asked me to get in contact with Moorfields Eye Hospital and explain that we'd been referred from Tenerife. Moorfields Eye Hospital said to come to the emergency entrance the next day.*

It all happened so quickly and before I knew it, we were at the airport waiting for our flight to depart. Sam and I have no memory of going home to our apartment in Roque del Conde to pack, nor how we got to the airport. I do remember using a payphone at the airport to call my mum and tell her why we were flying home, but I don't remember what she said, nor can I recollect being on the plane or arriving at my parents' house in Essex.

Sam phoned his parents, who were living in Hertfordshire at the time, and explained to them what was happening. They drove to Essex early the next morning so they could come to the hospital with us.

MOORFIELDS EYE HOSPITAL

22ND NOVEMBER, MORNING, 2004

*T*he next morning, we went to Moorfields Eye Hospital - me, Maisy, my parents, Sam's parents, my sister, Tina, and her husband, Kevin.

Tina translated the Spanish medical notes to the receptionist then we all sat waiting in the emergency area waiting for Maisy's name to be called. The hospital in Tenerife had advised us that there were only two eye specialist hospitals in the world, Moorfields and a hospital in Canada!

When Maisy's name was finally called, my sister, Tina, came into the room with me, Sam and Maisy. The young doctor who looked at Maisy's eyes was from the triage unit and said it looked like glaucoma. I remember looking at Tina and Sam knowing we were all thinking the same thing - glaucoma can be fixed with the right treatment!

The doctor disappeared for a few minutes. When he came back, he said he wanted another doctor to have a look. The second doctor looked at Maisy's scan photo and said he was unsure what the spots were on Maisy's eyes and that we needed to see a specialist. He sent us back to the waiting area again with the rest of our family.

The next time we were called, Maisy, Sam, Tina and I were shown to a door where a doctor was waiting outside for us. He told Sam and I to come in alone and to leave Maisy with my sister. My heart stopped. I knew then that this was serious. He hadn't even asked to examine Maisy's eyes.

As I entered the small box room, I noticed the doctor's worried look. As we sat, I could see Maisy's scan photo on his desk. He introduced himself as Dr Andrews. It seemed an eternity until he spoke again. When he did, he spoke slowly, eyeing each of us in turn.

'I'm afraid I don't have good news for you,' he said. I felt the room caving in on me until all I could see was his mouth moving, forming the words I had dreaded.

'Maisy has a very rare eye cancer called Retinoblastoma. It's a children's cancer that they're normally born with.' He explained that he'd never met a child with this cancer, only studied it at university. He continued to say that there's not much treatment available for this type of cancer.

I don't remember asking him any questions. I think Sam and I were in shock, and the doctor made it quite clear to us that there was not much that could be done to help Maisy.

He opened the door for us, and we left in silence. I was so upset and kept thinking, 'Was it Sam or I that passed this cancer to her? Did I do something wrong whilst pregnant? Did we do something wrong? Why us? Why Maisy? Is my daughter really going to die? Maybe the doctors had got it all wrong? Was she going to be blind?'

A MEMORY I WILL NEVER FORGET

22ND NOVEMBER, AFTERNOON, 2004

I remember thinking I wished it was me that had the cancer so she could live a happy healthy life and I could take her pain. When we walked out of that room, I remember Tina was waiting outside the room holding Maisy. I mouthed the words to Tina, 'she has cancer.'

I think Maisy put her arms out for me to take her, but I couldn't even look at her. I felt so sad and guilty.

We were then shown to a larger room by a nurse and the same doctor told us he was going to call the rest of our family in, so he could explain it to them too. I sat down next to Sam at the end of a large sofa as my family all started entering the room. A nurse entered and I could see she was filling up with tears. My mother-in-law, Steph, gave her a hug.

The doctor came in and explained to the rest of the family what he had just told us. I remember my dad and Tina firing off questions. We all wanted to know the prognosis, if there was any treatment, but at the same time we were all in total shock

The doctor didn't even mention possible medications or treatments that might help Maisy. He really had no idea about this cancer and so we were left to assume the worse - that Maisy was going to die or lose her sight.

Memory from Tina: *We waited anxiously to see the doctor and when we did it was awful news, I remember the doctor seemed almost excited about Maisy having Retinoblastoma as she was the first child with it he had ever seen. He gave us no hope and devastated our lives, I will never forget that day. We were all crying and trying to take it all in, but also in disbelief. Kay screamed out and ran to our dad, Colin. They hugged and both cried. I went to phone my other sister, Paula, as she was in London with friends. I told her the devastating news and asked her to come and meet us at the hospital, which she did almost straight away.*

We were told that we'd receive a call in the next few days from the Royal London Hospital then walked out of the room in silence or sobbing, all in shock. I was so sad I couldn't speak. All I could think about was that my beautiful baby was going to die.

Memory from Paula: *I remember getting the phone call from Tina to say it had been confirmed that it was cancer. I remember leaving my friends in London and crying all the way in the taxi to the hospital. I think I got it all out of my system so I could be strong in front of Kay and Sam. It was an awful and stressful time for everyone.*

I do remember that we stopped on the way home to buy pie and mash... strange the things you remember.

The pie and mash idea must have been Paula's idea as she has to eat it every time she comes to Essex.

Memory from my mum: *Tina was driving, and Kay was sitting next to her crying. At the traffic lights, Tina took her hand off the steering wheel and stroked Kay's arm. Steph and I were in the back of the car with Maisy in her car seat both crying our eyes out!*

Memory from Tina: *It was an awful journey home. Kay was broken, and we were all trying to be strong.*

When we arrived back at my parents' house later that afternoon, I went into their bedroom and shut the door. I made two phone calls to each of my best friends, Toni and Natasha and explained what the doctors had told me. They both cried with me. Sam and the rest of my family were all downstairs with Maisy. I remember not wanting to go down as I had nothing to say, and just wanted to cry without them all seeing me upset.

THE FOLLOWING DAY, my mum and I took Maisy on her first bus ride to the local library at Hilldene shops in Harold Hill. I awoke that morning desperate to read books on cancer so I could understand more about it.

At the library I couldn't find one book that I thought would help me understand more about children's cancers. I asked a librarian if there were any more books about children's cancers, but she said that was all the library had. I still carried on looking, desperate to find a book detailing a similar experience of what I was about to go through. The only book I could find that was close was Gary Lineker's, which I read within a few days. His son had leukaemia and survived. Obviously though, it's a different cancer to Maisy's and it didn't make me feel any better about our situation.

We stayed in at my parents for the rest of day playing and watching TV, and my dad drove to get us all fish and chips from the local chippy for dinner that evening. Maisy seemed fine, still happy and playing, though her eye looked red and sore.

6

ROYAL LONDON HOSPITAL

23RD NOVEMBER 2004

*T*he next morning a nurse from the Retinoblastoma clinic at the Royal London Hospital rang to tell me that there was a ward for children who have Retinoblastoma and treatment was available. She said that Maisy would need to be put under anaesthetic so the specialist team could thoroughly check her eyes and that it would be a long day, so to be prepared to wait.

I felt some relief, at least there was hope, but we had no idea what treatment Maisy would have to face. One thing I did know was that this wasn't going to be easy and that we were in for a long journey.

25TH NOVEMBER 2004

We went up to the Buxton Ward on the fourth floor and waited to be buzzed in. There were a few of us that day Sam, his parents, Steph and Richard, plus my sister, Tina, and our parents. The nurse showed us to a cot bed on the ward. It had curtains either side, and two chairs next to the bed. This was to be our private area for the day. It was only small, and there were too many of us to all be there at once, so the family took it in turns to wait outside in the corridor.

The ward was very long, lined with children sitting in their cots, and at the very end there was a bright and colourful children's play area.

We were told Maisy was sixth on the list to be called that day. Maisy wasn't allowed to eat so we had to try and entertain her for the next few hours whilst we waited. Considering she must have been starving, she was still happy. Because Maisy was not allowed to eat, I felt guilty eating, so I went hungry too.

On one hand I felt the need to talk to the other parents and ask them questions and look into their children's eyes to see if they looked like Maisy's. But on the other hand, it felt too early to start talking to other families in the same situation as us. As much as I wanted to speak to parents to get some hope, I knew I wasn't strong enough to talk about it yet without getting upset.

A nurse came and put a plastic tag around Maisy's wrist which stated her date of birth and her hospital number, 01405714. I still have this tag, along with most of the plastic bracelets that Maisy had to wear throughout her many treatments.

Every now and then the nurses would come over and check on us and give us an update on the list and an estimate of how much longer we'd have to wait before she was seen.

We were also visited by the play specialist who introduced herself as Caroline. She had a chat with us, asked how far we had travelled that day to be here, and said we were welcome to go and sit in the play area or to take some toys from there and bring them back to the bed area if we wanted. I asked Caroline if she could get Maisy a few toys to play with as I didn't want to leave her side.

Eventually, Dr Kingston, who was the paediatrician, came to check Maisy's chest and heart, and asked us a few questions about her health. She worked alongside Mr Hungerford (the specialist) and explained that we would be seeing them both again later this afternoon.

After a couple more hours of waiting a doctor from the Retinoblastoma team visited and gave us a consent form to sign. This made my eyes well with tears as we were no longer in control. All my faith and hope were with this team of specialists to keep our daughter alive.

The doctor advised that Maisy was next on the list to have her eye drops and then she would be called to the theatre room when the team were ready to see her. I felt sick. Sam and I agreed that I could take her, or maybe I just said I would, I can't remember. I just know that I needed to stay with her.

A nurse came to get us shortly afterwards and we walked along the ward near to the waiting room where they explained they will be putting eye drops in both of Maisy's eyes. I had to lay her down on my lap and hold her head still whilst the nurse put the drops in. She hated it and cried. We were then told to return to our bed and a nurse would check on Maisy soon.

When she did, Maisy's pupils were huge, which apparently was a good thing. Maisy's name was called, and I picked her up from the cot and followed the doctor through double doors. I already felt like crying; even as I'm writing this now, I have tears in my eyes. I was trying to be strong, and Maisy obviously had no idea where we were going and what was about to happen.

We entered a room and were greeted by a doctor and a nurse, who explained that they were going to place a mask over Maisy's mouth and nose and then count to ten while she fell asleep. The nurse was blowing bubbles to distract Maisy as she was getting irritable, probably starving and wondering what was happening.

I had to lay her in my arms while the doctor placed the mask over her mouth and the nurse and doctor both started counting to ten. I could feel the tears coming. It is such a horrible experience to have to do this to your baby. After the count of six, she was fast asleep, and I laid her down on the bed and left her in the care of the doctor. I left the room sobbing, my tears continuing to flood down my cheeks all the way down the corridor, out of the main doors into the play area. I could see other parents sitting with their children and felt such empathy for them all.

Maisy was the only new case that day at the hospital. Little did I know this was the first of many anaesthetics and an experience I hated every time but I always wanted to be the one that took her in that room so I could leave with the knowledge that she was asleep.

My family made sure I had lunch in the canteen, and I knew Maisy would be allowed to eat too when she returned so I no longer felt guilty by eating. I didn't stay long though as I wanted to get back to the cot area so I could hear when Maisy's name was called. Waiting was horrible, lost in my own thoughts, imagining the worst.

Maisy had been gone for almost an hour when I finally heard her name called.

I followed the nurse to a small room where Maisy was crying in a cot, her sweet little face puffy and red. I picked her up and gave her the biggest cuddle and told her that she had lots of food waiting for her. I think she was just happy to see me.

We walked back to her bed and my family all took turns to come and see her. I remember her sitting in her cot bed eating a cheese sandwich, a packet of Quaver crisps and a KitKat.

The nurse came and said that we would have to stay until the specialists were available to see us. There were still two children yet to been seen by the team, so we knew we were in for another long wait.

Eventually, Sam and I were called into a room where we met the specialist, Mr Hungerford. He was the nicest man, very reassuring, while Dr Kingston was so gentle. He said he had been a specialist in Retinoblastoma for many years, so Maisy was in the right hands. I completely trusted him - we had to.

Mr Hungerford explained that his team had done a detailed investigation of Maisy's eyes and had found a very large tumour in her right eye, with total retinal detachment, plus one large central tumour and a smaller tumour in her left eye. As there was no prospect of salvaging any useful vision in the right eye, Mr Hungerford recommended enucleation, or removal. The examination showed that the tumour had extended into the choroid, the vascular layer of the eye between the retina and the sclera that contains connective tissues. Mr Hungerford continued to explain that the tumours in the left eye would need to be treated with both chemotherapy and cryotherapy (used to freeze tumours).

He told us that the team had already used cryotherapy today, but they hoped they wouldn't have to keep using it as there was a risk it would cause loss of vision in that eye too.

I assume Dr Kingston also talked about the side effects of chemotherapy, but my brain had shut down. I was still trying to get my head around the fact that she would have to have her eye removed followed by six months of chemotherapy.

The team also said that they had done a test to see if the larger tumour in her right eye had spread to her brain, but that we would have to wait up to two weeks for those results. More waiting! I tried not to think too much about this, but obviously it was still a worry for us all and something that was in the back of my mind constantly, though I never let myself think the worst. I told myself I'd worry about that if and when I had to.

Dr Kingston also informed us that Sam and I would be tested to see why this had happened to Maisy. She asked if I had had a normal birth, if anyone else in the family had had Retinoblastoma, and if there were any kind of complications during my pregnancy.

My answer was no to all these questions. I told them that no one in our family had ever had cancer, but I still felt sick at just the thought that Sam or I had somehow been responsible for giving this to Maisy.

We all left hospital that day still sad, but a bit more positive as we now knew the hospital were going to help our Maisy.

My mum called Paula, my sister in Tenerife, that night to explain what the doctor had said. Because we had been told we'd have to stay in England for six months, Paula said she would clear out our Tenerife apartment and put everything in storage. Our dog, Lola, was being looked after by my sister and uncle Tom, but she was an absolute nutcase and was driving Tom mad as she didn't listen to him, so he'd arranged for her to stay with a friend. We spent a quiet night at my parents, but Maisy was very irritable, which was no great surprise after the day she'd just had. My dad took her into the kitchen and opened a cupboard to see what he could occupy her with. He found a box of Oxo cubes which he rattled, and Maisy loved it. My dad would then do this most nights with Maisy. She never seemed to get bored holding the Oxo box and rattling it. Simple pleasures!

Memory from Paula: *When I was called to be told Maisy had to have her eye removed, I remember feeling so sad as she was so* *small and seemed oblivious to what was going on. I flew back a few times from Tenerife to Essex over the next few months so I could see Maisy, but my family were always keeping me updated on everything.*

7
BACK AT MY PARENTS

2004

$\mathcal{B}$ack at my parents' house I felt so sad. However, it was nice to be away from the hospital and back home! That night, Sam and I lay in bed, quietly dealing with it in our own ways. He assured me that everything was going to be okay, that Maisy would be okay, but deep down we both knew that we had no idea what would happen.

The next few days were spent with my parents, and visits to my sister's house to see Maisy's cousins, Isabella and Daniella. There was only six months between Maisy and Isabella, while Daniella was seven. Due to us moving to Tenerife a few months before, we'd not seen them, so it was lovely to spend time with them.

I remember one night I was in the bath feeling sad and Daniella came in for a chat. She wasn't there long as I wasn't very chatty, so she left. When I got out of the bath and sat on the side, I had a cry. Daniella saw me upset and shouted to her mum, 'Auntie Kay is crying!' I remember Tina coming up the stairs to check on me, she was always such a great support.

I found it hard being around family at this time, even

though I wanted them all to be near me. I didn't want to talk and kept my feelings to myself, as I'm sure they all did too.

One morning the doorbell rang. It was the next-door neighbour, Ann Terry. We always had a lovely relationship with next door, my older sisters were friends with their daughter, and I baby sat her grandchildren and played with them whenever they visited their nanny Ann. I wasn't in a good place at the time and wasn't in the mood to speak to anyone. Ann told me that she'd been to church and she and her friends had prayed for Maisy. I smiled and said thank you, but I don't believe in God. If there was a God, why would he allow innocent children to be so poorly?

I also remember receiving a phone call that week from somebody in the neighbourhood. They said they'd been given my number from the hospital and was advised to contact me to see if I needed counselling. Straight away I said no, and the conversation was over. I never heard from them again, but maybe if they had contacted me further along into Maisy's treatments, I'm pretty sure I'd have taken up their offer.

We spent our days at my parents' house watching TV, playing and having cuddles, with the odd walk to the shop with Maisy in her push chair. Tina would pop in most days for a cup of tea as she was working locally at the time. Rita, my sister Paula's best friend, would also pop in every now and then for a cuppa too, and to make a fuss of Maisy.

My family were all an incredibly supportive, especially Tina. I couldn't have got through this difficult time without her. She was my taxi driver for one! I could drive, but I didn't own a car and I didn't want to take Maisy on trains to get her to her hospital appointments, so Tina was just always there. She could sense when I was sad and would always be the chatty person trying to make a joke or offering to take Maisy for a walk if she knew I needed to process what was happening or what I was being told by a doctor.

We were all dealing with the pain of what Maisy had to go through, but I didn't want anyone to worry about me too so I tried to not cry in front of them, even though I couldn't help it at times. Maisy had no idea what was going on and I still felt guilty. But all our energy had to focus on getting Maisy well and hoping that she would fight this cancer, so I made sure I did my best never to cry in front of her. She was so little and never understood and was too young to ask any questions.

Parking was always a nightmare near Royal London and Great Ormond Street hospitals. We'd always have to buy a parking ticket and then Tina would have to keep track of the time and go back to the car and buy another ticket for us to stay longer. Sometimes she was gone ages because she couldn't remember where she parked the car, or she'd got lost finding her way back to the Buxton Ward.

I remember once we were really cutting it fine. We were being discharged from Great Ormond Street and I knew our time had nearly run out on the ticket. But we chanced it, and then ran with Maisy in her push chair, but was too late, and the dreaded ticket was already pinned to our windscreen.

Shortly afterwards I was told by the hospital that I could apply for a disabled badge, which helped us immensely, well, Tina more than us to be fair!

8

EYE NUCLEATION

NOVEMBER 30TH 2004

*T*he night before her operation I couldn't sleep. I kept looking at Maisy and feeling so sorry for her, wondering what she was thinking, and having horrible thoughts about how they were going to remove her eye. I also worried what she would look like after, and why again this was happening to her. I wished I could take her place.

1ST DECEMBER 2004

We sat waiting in Royal London Hospital's Grosvenor Ward reception, an overnight bag by our side. Sam and I had been told that we could both stay, but only one of us could sleep on the ward with Maisy, the other parent had to bed down in the family room.

The nurse showed me, Sam, Tina, Steph and Richard, and Mum and Dad, to a bed at the end of the ward next to a wall. I sat Maisy in the cot bed playing with some toys given to us by the ward. She was happy, oblivious to what was about to happen to her today.

A nurse called Beverly took Maisy's temperature, asked us

a few questions, and advised us a doctor would be over to visit us soon. When the doctor arrived, he explained that after he's removed the left eye, Maisy will be fitted with a plastic shell to keep the eye socket open. The doctor gave me yet another consent form to sign, and we were told to wait for her to be called.

At midday, Maisy's name was called. With Maisy on my hip, I followed the nurse to a room. I had to pass her to the nurse as I wasn't allowed in. I was upset as I'd assumed I'd be able to stay with her until she was asleep like last time.

The nurse told me she'd be a couple of hours and then they would wheel her back in a cot bed. I walked back slowly and tearful as once again she was in the hands of the doctors, and it was out of my control.

I checked my watch so I could track the time and hoped that Maisy was okay. The next time we saw her she would only have one eye. It was a horrible feeling.

We all went for a walk to get some food at the canteen downstairs and to have a break from sitting on the ward. I didn't want to stay long as naturally I wanted to be there for Maisy when she returned.

Back on the ward we sat waiting, hoping she was alright, and that she'd be back soon. I couldn't speak as I fought back the tears. All I could think about was Maisy.

After more waiting and staring at the ward doors, a cot bed was pushed through. It was her. She was lying on her back sound asleep. A huge bandage was wrapped around her head covering her eye socket, but she was okay. She was alive.

The nurse said everything went well with the operation and that a doctor would be coming to speak to us all soon. She said that Maisy had been given pain killers and will need a good sleep.

We all sat watching her sleep, all in our own thoughts. I

remember wondering what her eye socket would look like with no eye and hoping that she wasn't in too much pain.

The doctors had given her paracetamol, ibuprofen, and handed me a seven-day prescription for Cephalexin to help with the pain. She must have been shattered from the operation and medication as she slept for a solid two hours.

Memory from Stephanie: *Shortly after Maisy returned from having her eye removed, Sam and his dad, Richard, both went outside and cried.*

I can't remember if I already knew that, maybe I did, maybe I just blocked it out as it was too sad to think about. Even now thinking about both of them outside having a cuddle and a cry is still sad to envisage.

When Maisy woke up, she was back to her smiley self. You wouldn't have thought she'd just had a major operation! It made us all feel happier seeing her happy, and the bandages didn't seem to be bothering her at all. She sat up and ate her lunch - a cheese sandwich, Quavers again, and a juice. I'm sure she would have been treated with sweets and chocolate too from her nanny's and Aunty Tina.

Memory from Tina: *Kay, you were so brave that day, I can't imagine how you must have felt.*

Later that afternoon we were visited by the doctor who advised us all that the operation had gone to plan, they'd removed all the tumour and were happy with the operation. This was great news to hear, and we were all thankful to the doctors and nurses.

That evening my family left to go home while Sam and I stayed at the hospital with Maisy as she needed to stay in for the night. I don't remember much more of this time at the hospital and I'm not sure Sam ever found that family room to sleep in.

ACCESS TO HOSPITAL Notes

When I started writing this book, I contacted Royal London Hospital to ask for all copies of her hospital notes. Within a few weeks they were sent to me in two folders and lay unread for nearly two months until I was ready to look at them. I knew by reading these it would give me more reminders of what I had forgotten - or tried to forget - as well as new information that I wasn't aware of. So when I was ready, I added all these new notes to help me write this story.

> **Hospital notes for this date stated:** *The tumour in her right eye was 1.8 x 1.6 x.1.2 cm almost filling the entire globe. Sections of the eye show endophytic retinoblastoma arising from the posterior aspect of the globe near the head of the optic nerve. Most of the tumour (90 per cent) is well differentiated but there are areas of necrosis (30 per cent) and widespread apoptosis. There is scattered mitotic figures but no inflammatory cells. Maisy was a weight of 8kg, her temperature was 37.5, Maisy was cuddled by a nurse when she woke crying, and she was given oral fluid and no vomiting after operation.*

During the operation the notes explained a lot of medical terms of how Mr Hungerford carried out the operation. It was very sad reading this although most of it made no sense to me due to the medical jargon used.

However, it did state significant bleeding and required a diathermy. I Googled the meaning of a diathermy: apparently it allows for precise incisions to be made, with limited blood loss, and is now used in nearly all surgical disciplines.

Hospital notes: *Maisy had a cannula inserted in theatre, and that when she returned from theatre, she did a large vomit. Bandages covered area, shows no signs of blood oozing from the eye, warming blanket.*

I also found a consent form for DNA testing signed by Sam from that day.

The notes also stated Maisy had her first tooth coming! Bless her.

The doctor visited us the next morning and said we could go home the following day. The bandages were left for the first 24 hours and Maisy was given Calpol every four hours to help her with any pain. The doctor visited again to remove the bandage and have a look at her eye. The eye was closed, bruised and swollen. I expected it to be open and sore, so I was relieved when I couldn't actually see the inside of her eye. I wasn't ready yet.

With the doctor happy, Maisy eating well and passing urine okay, we were discharged. I called Tina asking her to come and pick us up and told Maisy the good news that we were going back to Nana's house. When I received the discharge letter the nurse advised me that I'd receive a call in the next few weeks from our local hospital at Harold Wood in Essex to have a false eye fitted.

It was so good to be out of the hospital and in the fresh air, and Maisy slept all the way home in Aunty Tina's car.

That night we had dinner together. Maisy had Calpol to help with the pain and then I put her to bed. It was nice to be back in my own bed again. I had a great sleep, and Maisy did too.

9

RECOVERY

2004

*M*aisy was recovering well at home. She continued to have visits from her cousins, Isabella and Daniella, and my best friend Toni. After a few days the bruising was disappearing, and her left eye socket was beginning to open. I could now see a little piece of clear plastic in her socket.

She was happy staying in and playing, and within a week the eye socket was completely open and not as red as I imagined it would be. I could see the muscles still trying to work the missing eyeball, but Maisy coped with it very well. She never tried to touch it, even though sometimes it looked very red and sore Instead, I'd give the area a wipe with a pad and warm water just to make sure it didn't get infected.

I didn't want to take her outside until she'd had her eye fitted as I thought people would stare. I couldn't cope with people looking at her and not knowing the truth of what she was going through. So, we stayed in and continued to have visitors, including Sam's parents who came to see Maisy every week.

Before all this happened, she only had a dummy at night,

which I was okay about, but now she wanted it more and more. I gave in as I couldn't bear to hear her crying, not knowing if it was because she was in pain or just because she was tired.

Her love of dummies grew to the point where we had four on the go. She'd have one in her mouth and hold one in each hand, and occasionally she'd even have two in her mouth and one in each hand. She was funny. When she slept at night, we would scatter all the dummies around her so if she woke, she'd be able to find a dummy within reaching distance.

I have a lovely photo of Maisy sitting in a plastic box that you would normally use to put toys in or use as storage. She was sitting in it, holding a plastic toy star that made noises when you shook it. Her left eye socket was all red and swollen but she had a huge smile on her face. She was happy, this life of constant hospital appointments was just normal to her, and she knew no different. I still felt guilty when looking at her though. I'd be constantly making a fuss of her and giving her so much love. We all did.

During this time Sam managed to get his old job back in London as a builder and returned to work. Although we were living at my parents, we still needed money for food and to help them with the shopping. His boss was lovely and gave Sam any time off he needed for hospital appointments. Most days if we were in hospital Sam would come and visit straight from work.

My mum was working at Bonus Print in Romford but due to the circumstances she was allowed six weeks off so she could come to all the hospital appointments with me.

THE HICKMAN LINE

9TH DECEMBER 2004

We arrived at Great Ormond Street Hospital's Lion ward where Maisy had an appointment to have a Hickman line fitted ready to start chemotherapy the next month.

The doctor explained how he would thread a line through two small incisions, one in her neck and the other above the nipple area. He also told us that he'd be taking a lumbar puncture and a bone marrow sample and although this sounded scary, they reassured Sam and I that she would be okay.

We stayed with Maisy playing with a few of the hospital toys that the nurse had given her. Then the doctor arrived, Sam signed the obligatory consent form, and we walked with the doctor to the theatre room. We didn't really know what to expect when Maisy returned, but every time she went under anaesthetic, I was always felt so worried that she might not return. When she came back, she had a small plaster on her neck and the Hickman line was covered by a bandage around her chest to keep it clean from infection. She still had the cannula in her hand wrapped up with a bandage. I could see she was irritable and tired, and wanted lots of cuddles.

We were later discharged, and Maisy was prescribed lactulose to help with the pain. The doctor advised that we'd have a house call from a nurse the very next day to take the bandages off and we'd be shown how to clean the line.

As promised, the nurse visited the next morning and gave me a blue folder with Maisy's name on. This was now her record diary that the nurse would write in every time she visited once a week.

The nurse removed the bandages from Maisy's chest and was happy with the Hickman line. It was strange to see it at first as the tube was literally just hanging from her chest with an attachment at the end. The nurse explained that this was how the chemotherapy will be given, and that they could take blood samples from the line too. Very clever! She advised that we need to make sure the area was clean from infections and to check on the line daily. Also, we were told not to get the area wet and only to give Maisy shallow baths.

That week we received a call from Royal London Hospital to say that the results had come back regarding the tumour in Maisy's left eye, and they gave us the good news that the cancer had not spread to her brain. As you'll understand, this was a huge relief! If the tumour had spread to her brain the chances of surviving were very low. I phoned Sam, his parents and my sister, Tina, to tell them the good news. My parents were at home with me at the time, so we had a glass of wine to celebrate then my mum phoned my sister, Paula, in Tenerife to update her on Maisy's progress.

One morning Tina drove me to the Harold Hill Clinic. I only remember this vaguely and I can't remember if I had to drop a letter off or make an appointment for Maisy but anyway, Tina pulled up outside and I run in and spoke to the receptionist.

Memory from Tina: *Kay came running out in floods of tears because the receptionist had been rude to her. I flipped, and left Kay in the car while I went into the clinic and had a good moan. I was annoyed they'd upset my sister and not even taken into consideration what she was already going through. I explained this while shouting at the lady and then turned round to see the whole waiting room looking at me. I even recognised a lady that was waiting, one of the mums from my daughter's school, so I gave a cheery 'hi' and left!!!*

We went to visit Sam's parents at their new house in Hinchingbrooke in Huntingdon. Richard, my father-in-law picked us up and we stayed for a couple of days. It was almost Christmas, so they had their tree up. I have some lovely photos of Maisy sitting by their tree in her Christmas pyjamas.

During this time, we also went to visit Aunty Emma and Uncle Chico for the day at their flat in Banbury. We'd not been to that area before, so we all went for a walk and had lunch at Emma's. I have a photo of Maisy standing up against their coffee table eating chocolate buttons given to her by her Aunty Emma.

11

CHEMOTHERAPY TIME

17TH DECEMBER 2004

I was so nervous when we arrived at Great Ormond Street Hospitals' Tiger ward. I didn't know what to expect and was worried how Maisy's tiny body would cope with the drugs. When we walked through the double doors, I saw a boy sitting on a chair playing a computer game. He looked about six years old and had no hair. I felt my eyes starting to fill up but did my best to stay strong and to not cry.

I couldn't help but stare at all the children as we were shown to the waiting area. There were so many sitting on the floor playing with toys or playing on the computer, and most of them had no hair. I felt upset that Maisy would probably lose her hair too. It was bad enough knowing that she was poorly and needed help, and I guess having to cope with her hair loss was just something else Maisy and I would have to deal with.

We were shown to a seating area and waited to see a nurse. I still sat gawping; although these kids were all very poorly, they also looked happy, smiling, playing and just coping with their problems. Which made me want to cry even more. They were all so strong. I wanted to hug them all and tell them how strong they were.

Two nurses took us into a room and checked Maisy's weight, temperature and chest while she happily sat on Sam's knee. The nurse told us that they didn't know much about Retinoblastoma and that all the children on the ward today had leukaemia. Both nurses asked us a few questions about it, and Sam and I told them all we knew.

They then explained that Maisy would be having two drugs fed through the Hickman line, one for four hours then the other for two hours. Mrs Kingston explained this to us originally, but I hadn't taken this information in at the time. The drug that Maisy would be having for the next six months was Etoposide, given as an infusion over four hours (common side effects include lowers blood count, hair loss, diarrhoea, abdominal pain). The other drug was Carboplatin and given over two hours (common side effects include lowers blood count, nausea and sickness).

It was all beginning to feel overwhelming; so much had happened to us and to Maisy, and this was just the beginning of six months of treatments.

We were shown to a small private room which had a single bed, a small TV on a unit, and a big, purple leather chair. We put our coats on the back of the chair and got ourselves settled before the nurse returned, this time with a machine on wheels. She plugged it in and pulled Maisy's top up and attached the tube to Maisy's Hickman line.

We watched as the medicine travelled through the tubes and into Maisy's Hickman line, she just sat there unaware of what was going on. What we didn't realise at that time was that we now needed to constantly follow Maisy around so she didn't get tangled up or pulled on the tubes. She was mainly only crawling around the bed, but after a couple of hours she started to get irritable, so we took her to the play area on the ward. I carried Maisy on my hips whilst Sam and my mum followed next to us wheeling the machine making sure we stayed close together.

It was nice to get out of the room and Maisy was happy to look around and see the other kids. She was wriggling to get down, so we sat her on the rubber mats and found some toys. Now and then I would look at the other parents and wondered how their child was coping with cancer and chemotherapy. But I never asked. I was still too sad to talk to anyone about what was happening to Maisy, even though I would have loved to have spoken to someone who was going through a similar experience.

Sam and I were called in to a room by the nurses, we left Maisy with my mum. The nurse explained that we would be seeing Dr Kingston here today and she'd be taking blood samples from the both of us, which would be sent to The Royal London Hospital for analysis.

Later that day our bloods were taken, and we were told we'd receive a letter in the post with a response. We both walked out of that room in silence, and never spoke about it to each other.

The possible outcomes of this test were:

a)   The test result may indicate that it is likely that the disease has been inherited.

b)   The test result may indicate that it is unlikely that the disease gene has been inherited.

c)   The test results may not be informative because of the genetic patterns in the family, or it may not be possible to identify any mutation in the sample provided.

THE DAY WAS SO LONG, boring and tiring, but we were soon back at my parents' eating dinner, and Maisy had seemingly coped well with the first session of chemotherapy.

The next day she was tired and didn't really want to eat anything except crisps, so I let her eat them. At least it was something. We spent the day having cuddles and watching her favourite programme Teletubbies.

Maisy continued to feel tired and not eating much for the next two days and really clinging to me. But soon after, she started to feel better and had more energy even though she still looked very pale.

12

HOME VISITS

2004

1 9th December 2004

At 8.15am we had a home visit from the nurse from Harold Wood hospital care team, she explained that she would be taking bloods from Maisy's Hickman line. I watched the nurse take blood, whilst Maisy sat on my lap. The nurse then flushed the line with saline and Hepsal to stop the line getting infected. The nurse advised me to check on the line for any infections and to clean it. Her white blood cells seemed a little low and the nurse advised me she will return again in the morning to check her bloods again. She gave me the blue folder that I needed to keep with me and take to any hospital visits so the nurses could communicate and write notes in it if needed.

20TH DECEMBER

The nurse visited early morning, Maisy had had a good night sleep and seemed fine in herself. Her bloods were taken and nurse was happy for us to stay at home... phew not another visit to the local hospital, I was beginning to feel like it was our second home!

I took Maisy for a walk to see my friend Clare she was living at her mum's house, only a ten-minute walk away. I was happy to get some fresh air and Maisy was happy being pushed in her pram. We had a cup of tea and a chat in her living room whilst Maisy was happy playing on the floor. It was nice to see a different face and listen to what they had been doing in their life, rather than me talking about hospital appointments, I was fed up with talking about it. Plus, I would get upset talking about it too as I was still struggling with why Maisy had this cancer and trying to be strong for her.

When I returned to my parent's Sam was home and was sitting watching TV, my mum had bought Maisy some bubbles. Sam sat in the arm chair blowing bubbles for Maisy, she loved it.

13

CANCER CHECK-UP

2004

The following week we had to attend Maisy's three-week check-up at The Royal London Hospital on Buxton ward. Tina drove me, Sam and my mum there. We were taken to a cot bed where we waited until it was Maisy's turn to be seen. We did our best to keep her occupied until then.

Maisy's first check-up was with Dr Kingston who weighed her and listened to her chest and heart – and thankfully, she was pleased with the results. She noted that Maisy's growth wasn't exactly where it should be, but she wasn't overly concerned yet. I'd noticed that Mrs Kingston was very gentle and kind with children. It must have been hard dealing with so many poorly little ones.

Afterwards I signed a consent form for an eye drop procedure and the nurse said they were ready for her. As soon as Maisy recognised the room, she became distressed, so I had to hold her down while they put drops into her left eye. She was crying during the process, but cheered up afterwards when the nurse gave her a 'You are Brave' sticker.

We walked back down the corridor to our little area, and

we showed Nana Hazel her sticker. Not long after, the nurse came to say that the team were ready for her. I followed the nurse through double doors and into the same room as the first time we visited. I sat Maisy on my lap whilst the nurse started blowing the bubbles and the doctor placed the mask on her tiny face. Within a few counts she was asleep, so I laid her on the bed and left.

I walked out of that room with tears streaming down my face. This never got any easier. My mum and Tina stood up when they saw me and said, 'Come on let's go and get a cup of tea and eat our lunch.' I could see the sadness in their eyes too, but they didn't cry in front of me. We'd remembered to bring more change for the vending machine this time so we all drank a lot of tea!

As we sat down in the adult waiting room, I wasn't particularly hungry - I felt too guilty that Maisy hadn't eaten today. But my mum insisted I eat something. We took our teas back onto the ward to our little spot by the bed.

It wasn't long until her name was called and it was time to go get her. When the nurse led me to her, she was awake and crying, but I was so relieved to see her alive. I always had a dread that something had gone wrong, and they were unable to save her. I gave her a huge hug and told her it was okay now, that mummy was here, and it was time to eat.

We'd sit and cuddle next to the cot bed until she felt well enough to eat, and sometimes she would sit and sob whilst eating her crisps. It never took too long though before she was her happy self again, although much clingier to me; I needed her cuddles as much as she needed them from me. We then had to be seen by Mr Hungerford which we knew would possibly involve another couple of hours waiting.

Eventually a nurse came over and said Mr Hungerford was ready to see us. Sam, my sister Tina and I went in this time. Even though it was a small walk to that room in that short walk I was worrying about what they were going to tell me today and hoping with all my heart that it was good news. Please tell me she's going to be okay!

Mr Hungerford calmly explained that the tumours had not grown, her left eye socket looked clear and that he was happy with how the treatment was going so far.

Yay! All good news and we could now all go home as it was a long day of waiting and occupying a very hungry ten-month-old. We were shattered.

That day at the hospital when we were in the coffee room, we found a newsletter called CHECT (Childhood Eye Cancer Trust). It had lots of articles about children with Retinoblastoma, and stories of families that had raised money for CHECT. There was also a true story about a child's journey with Retinoblastoma. That week my mum signed up, as did Tina and Steph. We continued to receive that newsletter in the post for many years after.

OVER THE NEXT three weeks we stayed in, mainly at my parents as Maisy still only had a shield over her eye and I hated it when people stared, so we didn't leave the house. I relied on visitors to keep me company and sometimes I'd take Maisy for a walk around the block for fresh air with Toby, our dog. Her cousins still visited so she was able to sit on Nana Hazel's carpet and play with her cousin, Isabella. I loved seeing her with her cousins as I felt she was missing out on having fun. I was also visited by my close friends Toni and Natasha who also had children of their own, as well as Rita, my sister Paula's best friend. We always had someone visiting which was nice and I was becoming stronger and more able to talk about what was happening with Maisy without getting too upset.

14
FALSE EYE

2004

I have no notes of this, and the hospital no longer have these on record to give me, so this is all I remember of this day.

Sam and I got dropped off at Harold Wood hospital by my dad. After a while a women called us into a big room and told us to take a seat at a table, on which lay a blue chest. She opened the lid and from inside dozens of eyes of all different shapes and sizes stared out. Sam and I laughed. It was a such a weird, surreal moment. We'd never seen anything like this, but it was really interesting. Sam and I were both asking questions about why the eyes were all so different.

The lady removed Maisy's plastic shield using a small tube that stuck to the plastic and then she dragged it downwards and the shield popped out. Maisy was not particularly happy about having it removed. The eye did look sore, we could see the inside clearer and could still see the muscles moving. She explained that she would be pouring a liquid into Maisy's eye, which would be left in for a few minutes to harden and then she'd remove it.

She poured a custard-like solution into a long tube until

Maisy's eye socket was full. After a few minutes the lady took out the shield which now had the hardened liquid attached to it. This was a moulding of her eye socket, and this would be made into an eye to look the same as her right eye... amazing!

Her original shield was placed back in her socket, and we went home, awaiting the call to tell us the new false eye was ready.

15

A CHRISTMAS AND NEW YEAR TO FORGET

2004

*I*t was coming up to Christmas, but Sam and I were not in a celebrating mood and our family all felt the same. My sister Tina invited us all for Christmas dinner at her house in Romford; she thought we should all be together considering what was going on at this difficult time, which was a lovely idea. Sam's parents Steph and Richard were invited too, as well as his sister Emma and her boyfriend Chico.

23RD DECEMBER 2004

Another home visit from the nurse. Maisy sat on my lap whilst the nurse took her bloods which were completely fine and normal. She then flushed the Hickman line with Nasaline and Hepsal to clean it, and an antibacterial wipe to sterilise the area. She wrote in her hospital folder that Maisy was currently well.

CHRISTMAS Eve

It was Christmas Eve, and we were at my parent's house. Fortunately, Maisy was not even a year old and was unaware that we were not in a mood to celebrate or pretend to be happy. We spent the night watching TV with my parents whilst drinking a few snowballs, my favourite Christmas drink and a tradition in the Lewis house.

CHRISTMAS DAY

I don't remember anything from that day or doing any Christmas shopping. We looked back at photos from this day when I was writing this book as none of us could remember much from that day. It was lovely looking at the photos of us all together and we also had my lovely Nanny Winnie and Nanny Rene with us all that day too. My sister, Paula, husband Tom, and Jimmi and Maxi had all flown over from Tenerife as well so it must have been a madhouse at Tina's that day.

29TH DECEMBER

At 10.30am we had a home visit from the same nurse to clean and check the Hickman line and take bloods. I mentioned to the nurse that Maisy had had terrible diarrhoea at least two to three times a day and that her eye socket kept oozing. There was no heat coming from the eye, and her temperature was normal, but the nurse made an appointment for me to get her eye looked at the next day at the day care unit at Harold Wood. She continued to clean Maisy's line and redressed the area. The nurse was happy with Maisy and we both waved her off from the doorstep. Maisy and I went back inside and sat on my parent's living room floor playing with the toys that friends and family had bought her as presents.

All I remember is that one minute she was happily playing, and then the next, her whole body started to go red. I put my hand on her head and she felt so hot. Suddenly she went into a fit, and within seconds, her body stopped convulsing and she was okay again. My dad called an ambulance and Maisy and I were taken to the Oldchurch Hospital in Romford. I told my mum to call Sam.

The ambulance driver was chatty and told me that his son lived a few doors along from my parents. He said there was a special ward at Oldchurch Hospital for children with cancer, which was where he was taking us. The nurses met us at the door and showed us to a private room. I sat Maisy on the bed. She was wearing her pyjamas. The nurse got a couple of toys for her, but she was too poorly to play. She lay on the bed whilst the nurse took her temperature and her blood counts. Her temperature was still very high, and the results of the bloods showed there was an infection in her Hickman line. She was given medication and we were told we'd have to stay overnight.

Sam arrived early evening with my mum and dad. He brought me and Maisy an overnight bag with clothes, and more importantly, food! Although the hospital fed us, when you're just sitting around in hospitals it's just so boring, so food helps. We were discharged the next day as her temperature had gone back to normal and her blood counts were all good. Little did I know that this ward would become our home... literally!

That night I gave Maisy a shallow bath and let her play with her Noah's Ark bath toys that my friend, Natasha had bought her. She loved it. When I bathed Maisy, I would have to tape the Hickman line around her back so it wasn't hanging in her way, and to stop it getting wet which could lead to infections.

New Year's Eve was approaching, but again none of us

were in the mood for any celebrations so we just stayed in and had a few drinks with my parents. I still felt so sad; I just couldn't bring myself to be happy until I knew that Maisy's tumours were all dead.

My sister's friend, Rita, kindly offered us her house to look after as she was going on holiday for a week, and she thought it would give us and my parents a break. So, we packed some clothes and walked to Rita's, a five-minute stroll from my mum's.

16

OLDCHURCH HOSPITAL

5TH JANUARY 2005

*M*aisy woke up early at Rita's house and looked tired and lethargic. By mid-morning she could hardly move. She looked so poorly and had no energy at all. It was horrible to see her like this, so I phoned Oldchurch Hospital, who advised me to bring her in.

I packed a small bag of food and clothes, and my dad dropped me, Sam and my mum at the hospital. The nurse checked her temperature and blood counts. They were really low, so low that she needed a blood transfusion. I found the thought of someone else's blood being put into her body so strange, but I knew it had to be done.

Maisy lay on the bed completely still and silent, looking very poorly., The nurses attached her Hickman line to another machine, and I watched as the blood travelled through a tube into her body. The transfusion took four hours, and the whole time Maisy just lay still, mostly sleeping.

Sam, my mum and I sat around the bed anxiously watching her; lost in our own thoughts. When she woke up it was like a new Maisy, happy and with so much energy. I have a photo of her in the cot bed with her nappy on her head, laughing and in great spirits!

Maisy was discharged the next morning, but we were taken directly to Great Ormond Street Hospital by ambulance as Maisy was due her second round of chemotherapy that day. Thankfully her temperature and blood counts were now back to normal. I was on my own this time with Maisy and mentally preparing myself for another full day at the hospital. We didn't wait long in our room before Maisy was hooked up to the machine and the drugs were fed through her Hickman line. We sat on the bed watching TV and eating junk food. I really needed a good dinner in my belly, and every now and then a nurse would check in on us and bring me a cup of tea, which was always lovely. After lunch Maisy started getting bored and so did I, so we ventured out, one hand on my hip holding Maisy, the other pulling the machine along with us until I sat Maisy on a play mat close to our room.

Maisy was crawling a lot more now, so I had to watch her every move, making sure she didn't become detached from the machine. Not long after lunchtime Tina arrived to give some support, then after the first four hours were up, the nurses came and found us and swapped the drug over for another two-hour stint.

We were nearly finished but I was so tired. Although six hours doesn't actually seem that long, when you're sitting around doing nothing, time really drags.

Sam came to visit after he had finished work, and on his way to the hospital he had stopped at Persephone Book Shop and saw a series of books about a mouse called Maisie. It was spelt differently to how we spell Maisy, but I remember it being a lovely book he'd bought. Sam bought a few more over the next few months from that shop, and I still have those Maisie books in my loft.

Finally, we were finished but I was then told by the nurse that Maisy had to return to Oldchurch Hospital as she needed more antibiotics. I wanted to cry. I wanted to go home and just have a break from hospitals.

I'd had enough. I was broken. I wanted it all to stop and for this nightmare to be over. I was so fed up with hospitals and remember sitting in the ambulance so angry and sad that this was all happening to us. It just didn't seem to be getting any easier.

So much for our break staying at Rita's!

We arrived back at Oldchurch Hospital where I thought we were just having more antibiotics and would then be sent home, but the hospital wanted us to stay in. Maisy was still her happy self, but my heart sank at the thought of another night's sleep in a chair on a ward.

My parents visited again along with Sam bringing us more clothes, and the hospital gave us dinner. Tina and Kevin also visited, and Kevin and Sam drove us mad by constantly playing the game, Bop It.

The next morning Maisy looked much better, and nurses discharged us with antibiotics that she could take at home. My dad came to pick us up and take us back to their house. I couldn't wait to get back home. Maisy was happy playing and crawling around the living room and kitchen. We ordered a Chinese takeaway, watched TV and put Maisy to bed early as she was shattered.

Over the next few days, we mainly stayed in at my parents' house with the odd walk to get some fresh air. Sam was still working full days with just the weekends off so at weekends his parents would visit. My mum would cook a dinner, or a big lunch and we would sit and chat while they spent time with Maisy. I think they wished they had lived nearer at this point so they could also visit when she was at the hospital appointments. I would always try and call or text them whenever she was taken into hospital, to give them updates. Sometimes I think I was quite short with them when they asked me questions about how Maisy was doing and what had been happening. I just didn't want to talk about it, still in a state of shock that we were all going through this. So, when they visited at my mum's I didn't want to talk about hospitals, I wanted to talk about normal family things. I'm sure they understood as I certainly didn't mean to appear rude, it was just that I was fed up with it all. I wanted it all to be over and for Maisy to be well.

I loved it when she had her cousins over to play, to see her happy and playing with Isabella and being a normal 11-month-old. My mum had a beaded curtain in her kitchen to hide the big freezer that was under the stairs. Isabella and Maisy would often crawl to the curtain and play with it, loving the noise the beads made when they hit against the freezer.

Maisy liked being outside at Nana's, so on the days it was not too cold, I would take her into the garden. She was happy sitting on their garden step that leads to the lawn and would kick her legs and watch Toby the dog run around.

Maisy seemed to be doing well, and the nurse still visited once a week for her checks but mentioned that they were concerned her growth was not where it should be.

NEW EYE

17TH JANUARY 2005

*T*oday I woke up excited and nervous as Maisy was having a false eye fitted at our local hospital at Harold Wood. After dad dropped me, Maisy and my mum at the hospital we waited about 20 minutes before we were greeted by the same lady that did Maisy's moulding.

She removed a plastic eye from a plastic bag and showed us. It looked amazing. I felt overwhelmed as I knew I could now take Maisy outside more. Maisy sat on my lap whilst the lady took the plastic shield out of her eye with a small plastic tube then popped Maisy's new eye in very easily. I did have to hold Maisy tight because obviously she didn't know what was happening and it can't have been a nice feeling having it fitted.

Her eye looked a little red and swollen from the fitting but at least she now had an eye and it looked better than I could have imagined.

The lady explained that I'd need to learn how to remove the eye safely to clean it. She gave me a piece of paper with a web link written on it and told me to watch it and to take her eye out every four weeks to clean it. I can't say I was looking forward to removing her eye, but obviously it had to be done.

I was then given a booklet called *My Pretend Eye*, a small book to read to your child so they could understand about false eyes. Maisy was too little to understand but I still read it to her most nights over the next few days and kept it for when she was older and was able to comprehend. At the back of the book, it explained how to clean the false eye too and we left the hospital very happy.

She sat happily on the bus on the way home and when we arrived at nana's house, I placed her straight into her highchair to have some lunch. I have a lovely photo of her sitting there with her first false eye, yoghurt all round her face, and wearing the biggest grin.

SOCIAL ISOLATION

2005

1 9th January
    We had a home visit from the nurse at 8.15am. She took Maisy's blood as normal and flushed her line with saline and Hepsal. Her white blood cells seemed a little low, so the nurse advised me she'd be coming again the next morning.

20TH JANUARY

Another home visit at 8.15 in the morning by the nurse from Oldchurch hospital. She did the usual checks and flushed her line through to clear any infections. Maisy didn't have the best night's sleep as she seemed irritable and uncomfortable, but the blood samples were all good and the nurse was happy, so she left us to it.

I gave Maisy cereal for breakfast, but she didn't want to eat it, she just wanted to be held. I could tell she was not herself, crying and clinging to me for cuddles and she had started to feel warm. I checked her temperature, and it was high, so I phoned the children's cancer ward at Oldchurch

Hospital who again advised me to bring her in. The nurse had only left less than an hour ago.

My dad and Sam were both at work so Rita, a family friend, picked me and Maisy up and dropped me off at the hospital. The nurse took Maisy's bloods again as I told them that the nurse said that they were low the day before, but they were okay this morning. They gave Maisy a dose of antibiotics and she stayed in a hospital cot bed most of the day sleeping, she had no energy at all. This hospital was becoming our second home!

We were kept in overnight, and Maisy was given antibiotics every four hours. By the time the doctor did his rounds early morning, Maisy's temperature was back to normal, and she seemed fine so we were told we could go back home.

However, the doctor said due to Maisy getting so poorly so quickly and too often, he advised me not to take her outside in public and not to mix with anyone, especially children. Her immune system was so low her tiny body was easily affected by any germs, and it was making her poorly. I was gutted for her. She loved seeing her cousins and I loved seeing her play with them.

Back at my parents' house I called my sister Tina and repeated what the doctors had said. We were both gutted. We agreed that if any of us felt poorly we stayed away from Maisy. I felt so sorry for her; she was going through so much and now she wasn't allowed to have any contact with other children, and limited contact with anyone else. I felt so sad.

When Tina came to visit it had to be a doorstep visit or a wave from the living room window. Daniella was only seven, so she didn't really understand, and I just wanted to give her a cuddle.

I think I became a little paranoid around this time. If

anyone did pop by, I immediately wanted to shield Maisy from them in case they had any germs. I was fed up with the constant overnight stays at the hospitals; I really felt that I couldn't cope with any more nights staying on the Harold Wood cancer ward.

19

A NIGHT WE WILL NEVER FORGET

21ST JANUARY 2005

*W*e were at my parents' house, Sam was home from work, and we decided to treat ourselves to a Chinese and watch TV. Whilst waiting for the Chinese, Maisy started becoming irritable. She didn't want to sit on the floor and play, she just wanted to be held. I was constantly walking around the living room and the kitchen with her to make her happy.

Our take-away arrived and my dad and Sam were filling their plates up with food. I sat Maisy on the floor with some toys to try and occupy her so I could eat my food, but while she played, she was whinging at the same time.

I'd almost finished eating when I had an instant feeling that something was wrong with her. My mum picked her up so I could finish my dinner and immediately Maisy threw her head back and started waving her arms like she was doing the backstroke. I shouted, 'Maisy's having a fit!' My mum looked shocked as she hadn't realised. Sam shouted to call an ambulance. My dad ran in the kitchen to phone emergency services.

I grabbed Maisy and lay her down on the floor. It was at

that point I realised she'd stopped breathing. Her small lips were turning blue. We were all in a panic and I was shouting at her to wake up. Sam blew in her face repeatedly. It was one of the worst experiences ever and something that we'll all never forget. We all thought she was dead.

Sam continued to blow in her face and slowly she started to come around. By this time the ambulance had arrived, and the two paramedics were placing a mask over her tiny mouth and nose. She was breathing, but only just. Sam and I went in the ambulance to Oldchurch hospital with her.

I sat in the ambulance and cried. It was horrible and very upsetting for us all. I felt so upset that my parents had also witnessed this, and that Sam and I were going through this. We were both healthy, and definitely didn't deserve this, and nor did Maisy. I still ask myself, 'Why us?' and I always will.

We were met at the hospital entrance doors and Maisy was taken straight through. Fortunately, her breathing had improved by now. They gave her a thorough check and didn't seem to know what had caused this as her blood counts seemed okay. I was convinced it was a side effect from the chemotherapy, but the nurse and doctors said they had not heard of this kind of reaction before and assured me it was not.

I can't remember what they gave Maisy and have no notes of this day to remind me, but again we had to stay there the night while they kept an eye on her.

I gave my parent's a call to let them know we were staying there, as I know they would have been sitting at home worrying. My dad told me Mum was really upset. Sam had tried to make a joke of the situation when Maisy had started breathing again. Sam had said 'Bloody hell Hazel! What did you do to her?' He was trying to make us laugh as it was one of the worst situations I'd ever been in, but my mum took it to heart. Sam didn't mean anything hurtful by it, he was just trying to crack a joke, but admittedly it was not the right time.

Sam and I slept on the chairs in the room and unsurprisingly didn't have the best sleep. We were discharged early the following morning as Maisy seemed well and the doctor still had no idea what had caused Maisy to fit. My dad came to collect us to take us back home again, but for how long this time we would never know.

On the way back we stopped at the petrol station on the main road in Romford. I was sitting in the front passenger seat and Sam was in the back with Maisy. My dad turned to me and said he thought he needed a new heart after witnessing Maisy have a fit. We all laughed but it broke me a little bit. We were all going through this together and it must have been so hard on everyone to watch, especially our parents. I wanted to lean over and give him a hug, but I knew it would make me cry. Our parents were not only worrying about their grandchild but also their own children – me and Sam. It's one of the saddest memories I have.

I gave my mum a massive cuddle when we arrived back at the house that night and told her that Sam didn't mean what he'd said and was just trying to make a joke out of a very bad situation.

We all sat down and watched more TV and no doubt my mum would have poured me a glass of wine. I think I needed it.

20
BREATH-HOLDING

25TH JANUARY 2005

*A*t 12.40pm we had a home visit from the nurse. Maisy's blood was taken, and her Hickman line flushed as normal. The nurse asked if Maisy had had anymore fits. I told her she that she hadn't, not since that night. The nurse was happy with Maisy's blood counts and with her current health in general, and I waved the nurse off from my mum's doorstep.

Later that evening Sam was home early from work. Maisy was on the floor playing but started to get the hump and cry. I picked her up and almost straight away she started holding her breath!

It happened so quickly. Sam blew on her face and within seconds she was okay again. It was as if it was her way of saying I can't cope, or I've had enough of this. My mum and dad were there again that day and for a few seconds we all panicked but then afterwards Maisy was okay again, as if nothing has happened. I remember going to the toilet upstairs and having a good cry on my own. I didn't want to cry in front of my parents or Sam, but it was so sad seeing our baby so poorly.

. . .

26TH JANUARY 2005

We had an appointment for Maisy to go under anaesthetic to check the tumours. We arrived at lunchtime knowing that we were in for a long day, so we came prepared with lunch and some treats for Maisy. Again, she wasn't allowed to eat, only drink, so between me, my mum, Tina and Sam we constantly kept her occupied and playing with toys so she wouldn't ask for food.

I signed the consent form that day and we sat and waited our turn. She took a liking to a plastic car that she could climb into, but then demanded me to push her up and down the ward. She loved it and got upset if another child wanted to have a go. We also sat with the play specialist, Caroline, and Tina and I got carried away with the arts and crafts. We both love anything arty, so we were happy!!! We got to make fresh Play-Doh which I hadn't made before, so I enjoyed it.

Another consent form signed, and a check-up with Dr Kingston. Dr Kingston did her usual checks on Maisy - her weight, height, chest and heart. She was also a little concerned about her growth, and noticed a slight heart murmur, but didn't seem too worried at the moment as it was quite common but she said they'd be keeping an eye on it.

Another long day but it was worth it. Mr Hungerford was happy with Maisy's progress, so although we left the hospital feeling shattered, we also left happy.

Hospital notes: *Maisy well and active but still has episodes of breath holding. Unsure why.*

21

MORE CHEMO

27TH JANUARY 2005

*M*aisy had her third chemotherapy session on the Giraffe Ward at Great Ormond Street. Tina drove us, and we were able to park directly outside the hospital now that we had our blue badge. In our room - we always seemed to have the same room every time - Tina and I asked for a cup of tea, and we put the TV on for Maisy while we waited for the nurse to arrive.

She was hooked up to the machine in no time at all and we knew we then had a four-hour wait until the drug was changed. We explained to the nurse about Maisy's fit, but she also had no idea why this had happened.

Whilst Sam and I were sitting with Maisy the nurse came in to say a young couple had arrived a couple of hours ago with their son who has been diagnosed with Retinoblastoma, and would we be kind enough to speak to them.

I felt much more positive about Maisy by now. She was doing well; the cancer was not spreading, and we were hopeful. I felt that we might be able to give the couple some hope too.

Tina stayed with Maisy and Sam, while I was shown to

the family room, where I was greeted by a young couple like us. I explained that Maisy was doing really well, and we were in a much more positive place. They asked a few questions as I could see the worry in their faces.

I hoped I'd helped Kellie and Dean and managed to give them some faith and hope. We said we'd stay in touch and hoped to see each other on a day ward appointment so we could chat some more.

Back in the room, we kept ourselves busy reading magazines, chatting and playing with Maisy and going for the odd walk around the ward. After the six hours were finished and Maisy's Hickman line was cleaned by the nurse and the dressing changed, we were on our way home. Maisy would always sleep most of the journey home, she must have been knackered.

Hospital notes: *Maisy was active and playful.*

When we returned to my parent's house, there was a letter addressed to me and Sam. It was from The Royal London Hospital and announced that after testing our bloods, there was no indication that we had passed this cancer to Maisy. The cells had split causing Maisy to be born with this cancer. It was a relief for us that we hadn't passed or caused Maisy to have this cancer, we were just very unlucky. The letter also advised that there was only a one per cent chance of this happening again if we were to have more children. I always wanted a big family maybe four children, and surely this couldn't happen to us again, surely this was enough bad luck.

That evening, Maisy again had one of her episodes of breath-holding as the doctors called it. She'd now had a few and we were beginning to recognise the early signs, always starting with a small cry. I felt like I could no longer let her cry at all as I didn't want to keep seeing her do it; it was horrible. This time I blew on her face and again she was back with us within seconds. I was so glad that Sam and my parents were there. I was starting to panic and thinking what if it happened when I was on my own with her and I couldn't wake her up, but I needed to call an ambulance and at the same time blow on Maisy. I told my family that they were not allowed to leave me on my own with Maisy just in case.

Most of the time when I was at their house, Mum or Dad would be there too, but occasionally they would pop out to the local shops together. Or my dad would be at work and my mum would get the bus to Hilldene shops. As from today we always made sure one of them was with me as I was so scared that if something happened and I wouldn't be able to get her breathing again on my own.

That night I lay Maisy down to sleep on a small bed we'd made up on the floor next to Sam and mine's bed. She was shattered and fell asleep very quickly. Sam and I also went to bed to watch TV as Sam was having to get up early to travel to London for work.

I WOKE up early and squinted as the first rays of sunshine reached through the curtains and fell on Maisy's arm. I shot straight up and woke Sam. Something didn't look right on Maisy's body, she looked red.

Sam, still bleary-eyed, thought I was overreacting as he couldn't see it! I climbed out of bed and leaned over her to get a closer look. She was covered in a rash from head to toe.

I immediately called the cancer ward at Oldchurch Hospital and explained that she had had chemotherapy the day before and was convinced it was a side effect. The nurses said it was probably something she'd eaten, and I needed to bring her to the ward. She looked so poorly and still so red and swollen, the rash all over her body, including her face. It was scary seeing her body that swollen and Maisy just lying there shattered.

At the hospital the doctor was also convinced it was something she'd eaten the day before, but I knew she hadn't eaten anything different from normal. I was still adamant it was a side effect from the chemotherapy.

Maisy was given antibiotics and we were left to stay with her in the room. I popped out to the play area to borrow some toys for Maisy and then we waited until the doctor visited in the afternoon. He told us that Maisy needed to stay in overnight as she needed more medication. I felt trapped and needed to get some fresh air while Sam stayed with Maisy.

It was Maisy's birthday soon, so I walked to Romford town centre, ten minutes away, to get her a card, some decorations and a present. I always felt guilty leaving Maisy, even though she was fine with Sam, so I didn't stay out long and returned with food and drinks to keep us busy for a few hours whilst we waited again.

Sam left early evening and got a taxi back to my parents' house. I put my pyjamas on and got Maisy ready for bed. Another night sleeping in a chair while leaning on Maisy's cot bed! Hospitals are so noisy at night especially on a children's ward. There are always children crying or screaming, and people walking up and down the corridor. I text Sam to update him and to say good night, and then tried to sleep.

We were discharged the next morning and returned home. I was exhausted and sat watching TV while my mum played with Maisy on the carpet. We said little as I had nothing to talk about apart from hospitals, and I was fed up with it all.

I sat Maisy in her highchair while me and Mum sat at the

kitchen table to have lunch. Maisy sat eating for a few moments but then she started to look unwell and pale again. It looked like her cheeks were developing a rash again. I checked the rest of her body and everywhere else was fine. We had only been home a few hours, but I phoned the day care to explain, and they asked me to bring her back in. I packed an overnight bag for us both, just in case, and my dad dropped us back at Oldchurch hospital.

I just wanted to cry but I didn't even have the energy for that. I'd had enough of hospital visits; it was so draining.

The nurse showed us to a room and told us Maisy needed more antibiotics. We had a large room to ourselves, and Maisy was happy sitting in the cot bed playing with some toys from the ward. The nurse then mentioned we would need to stay over again! Another noisy night sleep, just great! Tina and Sam brought us some food that night and stayed for a while to give us some company.

Maisy would fall asleep quite easily when she was at the hospital, but she was always on medication, so that helped make her drowsy. I'd often sit and stare at Maisy wondering what she was thinking, and how her body was coping on the inside. I'd be in and out of sleep most of the night, constantly waking to see if she was still breathing.

The next morning Maisy still looked ill, and the doctor said Maisy's white blood cells were low. She was given more medication and we were told she'd need to stay another night.

I was absolutely gutted as it was her first birthday the very next day. This was not how I imagined she would be spending her first birthday.

22

MAISY'S FIRST BIRTHDAY

31ST JANUARY 2005

*A*s soon as Maisy woke up and I give her lots of birthday cuddles and sang to her. Sam and my parents visited that morning during visiting hours and brought their presents for her to open. I'd asked Sam to bring a cake, which the nurses kindly brought to our ward and sang happy birthday to her. Luckily, Maisy was too young to understand, which was a good thing. At least she'd never remember any of this.

Finally discharged, we went back to nana Hazel's house the next day. Maisy's cousins came for a visit at the window and dropped her presents on the doorstep as she was still susceptible to infections. Sam and I had bought her a big push-along car for her birthday as it was very similar to the car she loved playing with at hospital. I have some lovely photos of her sitting in it.

When we gave her the new car, she was more than happy opening the door, climbing in, shutting the door and just sitting in it. Sometimes I would push her around the block in it, or to the shops, or to walk Toby the dog. She was still unsteady on her feet and couldn't reach the pedals, but she loved being pushed around in it.

We ordered a Chinese takeaway to celebrate that night - my mum and dad loved a Chinese! I gave Maisy a warm shallow bath so she could have a play before bedtime. I always slept better at my mums, although I'd always wake in the night and check on her. I was always worried that 'she'd stop breathing, or have a fit, or her drugs would make some new side effect would appear.

All we seemed to do was reward ourselves with a Chinese takeaway. Maybe this is why I no longer enjoy Chinese food. My first choice now would be an Indian.

A LETTER ARRIVED today from the NHS Clinical Genetics team explaining about genes and the way we grow and develop.

I learnt that we have many thousands of genes and have two copies of nearly every gene. Normally we inherit one copy from each parent and pass one copy on to each child. We all have several genes that have a misprint in them, and usually these are paired with a normal gene, which overrides any effect from the altered one, so we're not aware of them. Some of these altered genes are inherited from a parent, others occur at the time of conception so are present in the child but not the parents.

Genes are packed together; these packages are call chromosomes. Each chromosome contains many hundreds of genes, and as yet we don't know exactly which genes are in each chromosome, but we do know that the Retinoblastoma gene is in chromosome 13.

This letter is dated 29th January 2005. I assume that now in the year 2023 as I write this, we can now find out which gene is in which chromosome.

The letter continued to explain that Retinoblastoma develops when there is a problem with both copies of the RB gene in a cell of the retina. Someone with bilateral retinoblastoma usually has one missing or altered copy of the Retinoblastoma gene in every cell of their body. A tumour develops if the other copy of the gene is damaged or lost. Unfortunately, the other gene does become damaged and so most people develop at least one tumour.

Some people with a bilateral Retinoblastoma have a family history of Retinoblastoma, but the majority do not.

It also informed us that as we have no family history of Retinoblastoma and our eye examinations were normal, the chances of us having another child with Retinoblastoma are about 5 per cent.

However, the chances of Maisy's children having it will be higher and she'll have a 50 per cent (or 1 in 2) chance of passing on the altered gene to each child. As a small number of people who have the altered gene don't develop a Retinoblastoma, the chances of having a child with retinoblastoma are a little less than 50 per cent. Both boys and girls can be affected.

The letter continued to talk about genes and said that they would be testing a blood sample from Maisy. If they're unable to find a misprint in the RB gene, then it would be possible to test both parents for that particular change. It was from Dr Elisabeth Rosser.

A FEW DAYS after Maisy's 1st birthday she took her first few steps. She'd been standing a lot more on her own but had never been quite ready to take that first step before. Sam and I were in the living room at my mum's, and she just did it. We made such a fuss of her, and she was so happy with herself. Luckily, we could shut the door of the living room, so we never bothered to buy a stair gate for downstairs, though Dad did have one fitted on the landing at the top of the stairs.

During this time, I'd begun to notice that her false eye moved sometimes. It went off-centre, which then made me upset thinking that people would stare at her. I contacted Harold Wood Hospital to tell them I wasn't happy with the eye as it kept moving, and they said they'd make an appointment for the prosthetic department.

23

HALFWAY THERE

9TH FEBRUARY 2005

*M*aisy was now halfway through her chemo treatment. A nurse came in the morning.

Nurse notes from a home visit: *Maisy unsettled. Bloods taken via the Hickman line then flushed with Nasaline and Hepsal. Exit site was cleaned with chlorhexidine and redressed. Maisy still slightly under weight.*

Later that morning Maisy had another episode of breath-holding, I picked her up as soon as she started crying as I had a feeling she was about to hold her breath. Her eyes looked like they were just about to roll, and I did the biggest blow in her face a couple of times, which seemed to work. I always just cuddled her afterwards and told her she was okay. I was still convinced, and still am to this day, that she held her breath as she just couldn't cope with what her body was being subjected to. She was now a year old and still so tiny; all those drugs being put in her small frame. It was sad thinking about what was happening to her, as she obviously didn't understand and was capable of speaking to me and telling me how she felt.

Maisy had all our full attention 24/7 as soon as we heard a moan or a small cry one of us would literally run to grab her to stop her holding her breath. Thankfully it seemed to work.

Whenever Maisy slept, I would constantly check on her, feeling her pulse to make sure she was still alive. I just had this worry that one day she would stop breathing for good.

I knew the six months of treatments would be hard, but I was not prepared for all the constant appointments and ambulance trips and overnight stays in hospital. I was also beginning to worry that Maisy was not coping well with any medications, due to them having so many side effects.

I raised my concerns to the nurses and doctors at any appointments we had, but they were not convinced all the side effects were from the chemotherapy. Either that, or they would say that they were unsure as to why her body kept reacting the way it did.

11TH FEBRUARY 2005

Sam, my mum, Tina and I sat waiting at Royal London Hospital for her three-week check-up. She was eighth on the list of children to be seen so we knew we were in for a very long day. To be fair, the doctors were trying to be as quick as they could as they knew the children hadn't eaten that morning.

Tina and I took Maisy to the play area where we sat craft making. Caroline the play specialist was there and always made time to have a chat with us, along with all the families that were there on the ward that day. Maisy always remembered the big, plastic toy car, and if there were no children using it, she would have me pushing her up and down the ward and around the play area.

We were visited by the Retinoblastoma team, and I signed the consent form. When we went into the room to see Dr Kingston, she told us that Maisy was the second child with this type of cancer who had not lost her hair. She also continued to say that she was amazed at how much Maisy could see from her left eye considering the tumours that were sitting on and around her pupil. It was so lovely to hear. I was so glad that she could see better than the doctors had thought, and obviously I was happy that Maisy's hair hadn't fallen out. She was a little miracle, and a fighter. I gave her the biggest kisses and cuddles when we walked back to the family to tell them the good news.

Whilst we were back in the waiting room, I saw Kellie and Dean with Luca, the couple we had spoken to at Great Ormond Street. It was lovely to see them. Kellie was there with her parents. I walked over to say hello and we introduced our mums. I think it was useful for my mum to have a chat with Kellie's mum. Luca, their son, didn't have to have his eye removed, although both eyes were affected. He was a cute little boy of a similar age to Maisy.

Kelly and I sat on the tiny chairs in the play area with Maisy and Luca on our laps and occupied them with some colouring. It was nice to have a chat and for us to talk about the two kids. We both knew how hard it was to see our babies go through this, and luckily, like me, she had great family support.

When it was our turn to see Mr Hungerford, I felt more confident and asked a few questions including, 'If the cancer was dead after the six months of chemotherapy, could it return?' His answer was that it could return anytime up to the age of five. That was not the answer I wanted to hear. I just wanted the cancer to be dead and for us to live a normal life.

I FINALLY HAD an appointment to see the prosthetics team at Harold Wood. We saw the same lady as before and I explained that I was not happy with Maisy's eye. I told the lady that it seemed okay for a few days and then would spin around. She advised us that she would take another moulding and make a new eye, as maybe it needed to be bigger to fill out the eye socket more. I was told we'd be contacted when the eye was ready to be fitted, possibly in a few weeks' time.

24

GIVING SOMETHING BACK

15TH FEBRUARY

*I*t was around this time that I decided I wanted to do something for charity and raise money for the Eye Cancer Trust. I asked a few families and friends and six of us decided to do a charity run. I set up a just giving page on Facebook and explained that we were all participating in The Flora Family Marathon. From the March 1st we had to run 25 miles between us and the last mile we would run together on the 26th of March. I contacted CHECT to ask if we could have any posters, medals, anything that had the CHECT logo on and to help us to get sponsors. They sent me a bag of goodies with t-shirts too.

My sister Paula's best friend, Rita, who lived in Harold Hill wanted to also organise a charity night to raise money. Rita and her friend Nicky contacted many companies to ask for free memorabilia, free balloons, free anything. Nicky even wrote a letter to *Eastenders* asking for any memorabilia or help. A couple of days after sending the letter, Nicky received a phone call from Joe Swash who told Nicky he would see what he could do and that he'd be in touch.

The date for the event was Saturday 30th April. Sam and I

hoped to be able to go and take Maisy, but she was still so poorly all the time. We still hadn't let her mix or meet any friends or family apart from my parents. I told Rita we would have to see nearer the time. A few days later Rita and Nicky bumped into Joe Swash whilst out shopping and had their photo taken with him.

18TH FEBRUARY 2005

Back to Great Ormond Street again for her fourth session of chemotherapy. The doctors also informed us that they wanted to do a brain scan on Maisy, to see why she was having fits.

Maisy was checked by the nurse to make sure she was well enough for chemotherapy that day. Her bloods were fine, the strength in her limbs was good, her chest was clear, so they gave her the green light.

After six hours of chemotherapy, we waited for the doctor to come and take us downstairs to the theatre room to have the brain scan. I remember going into a lift which went down to what felt like the basement. It was quite dark and cold down there. When I saw the scan machine it looked quite scary as it was huge. I remember her laying still, but I'm still not sure how they managed to scan her with her being so little.

21ST FEBRUARY

Nurse's home visit notes: *Maisy was unsettled, bloods were taken via Hickman line, line flushed with Nasaline and Hepsal, exit site cleaned with chlorhexidine and redressed. Still slightly under weight, an appointment was made for smart site to be changed as per four-week policy.*

· · ·

9ᵀᴴ MARCH

We arrived for another check-up at Royal London Hospital on the Buxton Ward. The nurses were all so lovely and chatty, trying to make us feel comfortable. By now they knew who Maisy was, and Caroline the play specialist would always come over for a chat.

Whilst we sat around Maisy's cot bed chatting and getting comfortable, I would always have a quick look at the other families and smile at them if they were looking my way. Although I never spoke to any of them, I felt their pain!

Our check-up with Dr Kingston went well. Maisy's growth rate was still below where she should be but to be honest it was no surprise with all the medication, she was having at the time. Her chest was nice and clear, and she could no longer hear the heart murmur.

Hospital Notes from Dr Kingston; *Her mother thinks that Maisy's vision is good and feels that she can see and recognise people across the room. On examination at the clinics, she was slightly pale, but lively. Her chest was clear and there was no external abnormality of the left eye.*

Mr Hungerford undertook an EUA, and I am pleased to say that there were no signs of recurrent disease in the right socket whist the tumours in her left eye all appeared inert and there were no new tumours.

More notes from Dr C Abdulla the consultant paediatrician: If all the tumours in her left eye remain stable and she is count recovered, she will be able to come to Great Ormond Street for her fifth chemotherapy.

· · ·

10ᵀᴴ MARCH

Maisy had her new eye fitted. The colour looked okay, and I was grateful, I really was, but it still didn't look perfect to me. I thanked the lady and left the hospital, but the more I glanced at Maisy on the way home, the more it looked completely different to her good eye. It made me upset. I know Maisy was little and she didn't know what she looked like but after everything she was going through, I just wanted her to have an eye that looked the same as her good eye. I was quiet on the way home and thought maybe her eyes will always look like this and that I had to accept it. Over the next few days her eye settled, although it still looked slightly different. I was just grateful she was here with us, and she was able to have a false eye at all.

25

CHEMO NUMBER 5

17TH MARCH 2005

*M*aisy's fifth chemotherapy session! It was just me today. Tina was working but told me to call her when we were finished, and she would come and pick us up. Sam planned to visit this afternoon too. So, my dad dropped me off that morning, my mum was now back at work, and I felt okay going on my own with Maisy, knowing that Tina and Sam would be there later today to keep me company.

I spent the day mainly outside of the room as Maisy was no longer happy staying in the room with the door shut for very long; she must have remembered that there were toys on the other side of the door. I was good at holding Maisy now and wheeling along her chemotherapy machine. We found a place on the mat with a few toys scattered around us to play with.

As soon as the nurse said we could go home I took Maisy to the waiting area on the ground floor of Great Ormond Street to wait for my sister Tina. I'd been on the ward all day and couldn't wait to leave and have a change of scenery. There was a small play area for the children in the waiting area, which included a bus that they could climb on and play in.

We were there for about 20 minutes when Aunty Tina arrived, strode over and whispered, 'That's Darius from Pop Idol.' I looked over and he was sitting not that far from me, but I hadn't noticed. Tina went straight over to him to say hello and told him all about Maisy. She asked him for a photo with Maisy sitting on his knee. He was friendly enough and we had a chat before we said our goodbyes. I later Googled why Darius was at Great Ormond Street. Apparently, he was there for the afternoon chatting to poorly kids on the children's wards.

On the way home Tina told me she'd spoken to Rita who was organising the charity night and a hall had been confirmed for the event. It was my old junior school hall at Pyrgo Priory in Harold Hill. Rita and Nicky had made small posters advertising the charity night and were asking business for donations or items to auction to raise as much money as they could. I just left Nicky and Rita to organise it and don't think I even offered my services; I was just too wrapped up getting Maisy through her treatments and getting her well.

My best friend Toni had asked me if she could organise a party for Maisy's birthday seeing as she was unable to celebrate it before as she was in hospital. Toni had contacts with the Salvation Army Hall at Petersfield Avenue and said there was a date available.

By this time, Maisy was doing okay, and she was coming to the end of her treatment, so we were all more positive and I thought it was a great idea and a lovely way to spend some time with family and friends.

26TH MARCH 2005

It was the day of our charity run. We all met at Lodge Farm Park in Romford. The runners were myself, Sam, Tina, her husband Kevin, Chico, my brother Gary, and my brother's best friend Paul, who was a runner. We set up a finishing line and the plan was to go to my sister's house for a BBQ afterwards. My niece Daniella joined in the fun too. We all set off together and did our run as we arranged, my mum, dad and Maisy were there for support. It was a nice bright dry day and my parents were holding and playing with Maisy whilst we all run. Paul was the first runner to reach the finish line. Paul raised £972 and together we raised all £2,257.71 for Chect.org.

28ᵀᴴ MARCH

Hospital notes: *Home Visit, the nurse stated that Maisy was well, bloods taken, line flushed and dressing changed.*

5ᵀᴴ APRIL

Hospital notes: *Home Visit at 8am, notes stated Maisy well, line flushed, bloods taken, ready for chemo Thursday.*

26

THE LAST CHEMO!

7TH APRIL 2005

*T*oday was Maisy's last chemotherapy session. I felt mixed emotions. I kept thinking what if the chemotherapy is not working and the tumours have grown, or more tumours have appeared. Was six months of chemotherapy enough? What happens next? Will she be okay?

My mum, Maisy and I arrived at the hospital and as normal were shown to the same room we always have, first door on the left as you enter the Giraffe Ward. I took out Maisy's lunch box and gave her some crisps while we waited for the nurse to return with the chemo. We didn't wait long, and I pulled up Maisy's t-shirt to help the nurse while she attached the chemo to the Hickman line. The nurse left leaving Maisy happily sitting on the bed eating her crisps so me and my mum sat down to eat our sandwiches as well.

Then Maisy started to cough, a couple of minutes after having her chemotherapy plugged into her Hickman line. I remember thinking it was strange as she'd been fine all morning with no signs of a cough or a cold. Soon it started to be continuous, and Maisy climbed off the bed and held on to the side of the bed, still coughing. She then started to become irritable and suddenly had a fit, her body growing redder by the second. Mum pressed the emergency button while I opened the door and shouted for help. Straight away a nurse came running.

Maisy was awake but very limp, her body and face, red and starting to swell. I panicked, looked at my mum, and could see she was getting upset too. We had no idea what was happening, nor why. There were now two nurses in the room, and they came to the decision to stop the chemotherapy. As soon as they unhooked the chemotherapy from her Hickman line the coughing stopped.

The nurse said to wait, and a doctor would come and talk to us. Maisy was on my lap, still looking red and swollen, and very upset. When the doctor came, he said that he wanted to take Maisy for a full body x-ray. They needed to scan her chest to check the Hickman line. I could see my mum was still getting upset, and she had to stay in the room while I followed the doctor to the x-ray room. My poor mum was then left worrying all on her own.

After the x-ray we needed to wait again to see the doctor with the results. It was worrying as I was thinking what if the doctors say she can't have any more chemo, then what would happen to her?

The doctor explained that Maisy's body was showing signs that she couldn't cope with any more chemotherapy. It was the carboplatin that was affecting her. He said that they couldn't give her anymore. I sat holding her so tight, tearful and rocking her. She was so upset and so hot, so I stripped off her clothes down to her nappy.

The doctor prescribed Puritan to stop the swelling and said the Royal London Hospital would be informed and that they would contact us.

We left there feeling so worried. Maisy was still looking red and swollen but at least we could finally go home.

Hospital notes: *Oxygen saturations had dropped to the low 90s, but a chest x-ray showed that the line was in the correct position and no abnormality could be identified in the lung fields.*

With the chemotherapy now stopped, we had to wait for an appointment at the Royal London Hospital for Mr Hungerford and his team to see Maisy and to see if the tumours were dead. It was a major worry. What if five months of chemotherapy were not enough? What if the cancer wasn't dead? What if it returns? This was all I could think about.

The next day the swelling had gone down, and Maisy was no longer as red, but she was still not herself. I phoned Oldchurch Hospital and they told me to bring her in to be checked. I packed an overnight bag (just in case) and some food, and my dad dropped us off.

Tests showed an infection in her blood, which required antibiotics. The nurse said we could go home for a bit if I preferred, but we'd need to return in a few hours for more antibiotics. I wanted to go home. I had had enough of hospitals. I think the nurse could see that I couldn't face another night sleeping there again.

So, for the next few days we were travelling to the hospital in the mornings and again in the afternoon. My dad, Kevin, my brother-in-law, and Tina all helped with ferrying us there and back. Although we were traveling a lot every day, at least we also got to spend some time at home. In less than a week the doctor was happy that the infection had gone and arranged an appointment to get the Hickman line removed as soon as possible.

. . .

11TH APRIL 2005

A letter from Elizabeth Price, the same letter that would have been sent to Maisy's local doctors, stated that: blood DNA from Maisy was screened, and the results showed that this RBI mutation was present in her germ line, which meant any children of hers would have a 50 per cent risk of inheriting this mutation, with close to 100 per cent penetrance.

It was sad reading those words, but I told myself not to worry about this at the moment as she was only a baby herself and by the time she was an adult there may be medical advancements that could overcome this.

As for Maisy's eye, some days it looked okay and in the correct position, while on other days it moved off-centre. I'd also noticed that when Maisy chatted to us or looked at me, she would always tilt her head, and I made a mental note to mention it to the doctor on our next visit.

15TH APRIL

Sam and I took Maisy to Great Ormond Street Hospital to get her line removed. She was called in to see the doctor at 9.20am and had to go under anaesthetic - yet another consent form to sign! I wasn't allowed in with her, so Sam and I went to the café in the hospital to get a cup of tea.

An hour or so later she came back, very irritable and upset so had lots of cuddles with me and her dad. It was so nice to see that the Hickman line had gone, the incisions covered by a plaster, one on her chest and one on her neck. I finally got her to have a sleep while Sam went for a walk and came back with another 'Maisie Mouse' book to add to our collection. She woke two hours later looking much brighter and had a cheese sandwich and a packet of cheesy Wotsits.

The nurse told us we could go home, and she gave me a

small white envelope. Inside was a photo of a Hickman line and a note that read:

Dear Maisy,
Here is a picture of your Hickman line for you to keep. Just think, soon you can have a deep bath and maybe go swimming!
You have been a star patient. Well done!
Take care
Lots of love
All the staff at the Day Care

I added this card to the album I had been making for Maisy, along with the rest of the hospital letters, hospital tags and photos I'd taken.

We left later that day with a letter explaining the after care of having the line removed. We needed to keep the wound dry for five days, and the stitches would fall off as it healed. If Maisy experienced any discomfort experienced, we were to give her paracetamol. They also gave her a Certificate of Achievement, signed by the staff at Elephant Day Care. Tina came to get us, and we went straight home, shattered.

27

MAISY'S BELATED BIRTHDAY BASH

19TH APRIL 2005

*T*oni, my best friend, was able to organise a party at The Salvation Hall on Petersfield Avenue. She and her mum did everything for us, including decorating the room with so many balloons and banners!

We only invited a few friends. Paula, my sister, flew over from Tenerife with Jimmi and Maxi, my nephew and niece. Maisy wore the same party outfit as her cousins, Daniella, Maxi and Isabella - a cream skirt, cream wrap cardigan with silver trimming and cream tights, which Paula had brought from Monsoon. They all looked so pretty, and I have lots of photos of them all in their Monsoon outfits.

We played musical statues, bumps, pin the tail on the donkey and pass the parcel. Auntie Paula brought a bubble machine, which the kids all loved. It was lovely to see Maisy smiling and having fun with her friends and family. We all sang happy birthday as we brought in a pink and white fairy cake. It was a lovely celebration, and I was really grateful to Toni and her mum.

Memory from Toni: *Kay brought me a lovely butterfly bracelet and a sparkly heart brooch to say thank you for organising the party.*

MAISY'S BASH!
SATURDAY 30th APRIL
FROM 7PM TILL LATE
BRING YOUR OWN DRINK AND NIBBLES
RAFFLE AND AUCTION
ALL PROCEEDS FOR MAISY ROSE

The night before the charity event that Rita and Nicky had named Maisy's Bash, I broke the news to Rita that Maisy was unlikely to be going as she was still too poorly, but I would let her know for sure the next day. I suggested that we could pop in and see the decorations before everyone was due to arrive.

Maisy woke up on the day of the event very happy. All day Sam and I were still deciding if we should take Maisy and stay the night, or just pop in and help people set up the decorations and just generally help out. By early evening we decided to take Maisy to see Rita and all the people that were setting up the hall. I wanted them to see Maisy and for us to say a big thank you to them all.

As we arrived it felt strange being at my old school, we walked along the side of the school until the open doors that led to the hall. We saw so many people that we didn't even know. There was a lady setting up a balloon display that she'd donated from 'Vision Balloons'. There was also a man carrying in toys and setting up the raffle area.

We found Rita and Nicky who were so happy to see us and to see Maisy. They introduced us to a few of the helpers. I could see a man getting dressed into a Bob the Builder outfit and someone was already dressed as Winnie the Pooh.

The characters came over to us to say hello and Sam held Maisy so she could see them. She wasn't sure if she liked them or not and didn't want to get too close to them.

There were so many people helping - it was really overwhelming. I had never been to a charity event before and didn't know what to expect. Soon people were arriving including my family. Sam said for us to stay as Maisy seemed fine, and if we stayed near the door the fresh air would help as she wouldn't be mixing too much. So, from the corner of the hall, where we stayed all evening, we listened to the raffle and auction.

I remember watching Kevin, Rita's husband, standing at the main doors on his mobile. Whoever he was talking too was obviously giving him instructions to bid on the auction. Kevin looked so professional, and we later found out that the bidder was my sister, Paula from Tenerife, who was bidding on a signed David Beckham football.

There were so many items up for auction, Rita and Nicky had done so well:

- West Ham signed football
- West Ham signed football shirt
- West Ham signed photograph
- West Ham signed top, signed by Trevor Brooking
- Teddy Sheringham signed photo
- David Beckham signed photo
- Tottenham signed football and tour tickets
- Tottenham signed football shirt
- Tottenham signed photo
- Robbie Keane signed photo
- Arsenal signed photo
- Arsenal signed photo
- Everton signed photo
- Wayne Rooney signed photo

- Ruud Van Nistelrooy signed photo, plus a Man United signed shield
- Raleigh mountain bike
- EastEnders' signed cast photos, plus Dot Cotton's brooch
- Two weeks accommodation in a 5* apartment in Tenerife, worth £1700
- McFly CD, and 2 tour tickets

Raffle prizes included: £100 voucher for various shops; assortment of children's gifts; family tickets including Romford Ice Rink, Romford Dog Stadium and Romford cinema; bottle of Baileys and box of chocolates; 100-minute sunbed session; signed Southend football, signed Celtic football; GMTV goodie bag; a course of sunbed treatments from BeautyLicious.

My friend Anita, her mum donated a fluffy horse, cutlery set, coffee set, candles, and an Indian warmer. The head teacher from Pyrgo Priory donated a smelly set, while Beauty Room donated £30 vouchers, and The Conservatory Hairdressers donated a full make-over.

I have many small notes and 'thinking of you' cards from this night. I also recently found a card from my old work friends, Natalie Talbot, Georgina, Becky, and Craig and Michelle, who each wrote lovely notes to me, Sam and Maisy, and they kindly gave us some money.

There was also a small card to us hoping Maisy continued to make progress from Lorraine, Peter and family.

We also had a surprise visit from Danielle Brent who starred in Bad Girls; she helped with the raffle and gave Rita some signed photo cards from some of the cast of Bad Girls. I kept these photo cards to show Maisy when she was older.

We didn't stay all night as Maisy started getting irritable, so we said a few goodbyes and left. I would have liked to have said thank you to everyone on the microphone, but I wasn't strong enough and knew I'd cry and not be able to say what I wanted to say.

A few days later Rita came over for a cup of tea and gave me some envelopes from donations that the following people had generously given:

- Phil the Fishman at Saxon King
- Christine and Richard Sees
- Elsie, Carol Russel's mum (Carol is one of my mum's best friends).
- Lil and daughter Gina - Lil was my grandad's girlfriend, he sadly passed away so he never got to meet Maisy, she would have loved him, as would my boys too.
- Mrs Sam Forrest
- All the staff and customers at the Alma Arms pub
- James Masterton and family
- Provident

Dot Cottons' brooch was sold for £100 to Rita's cousin who'd bought it for her daughter as she was a big Eastenders fan.

The charity event made an article in the local Romford Recorder. A kind lady named Margaret Kelly who lived in Romford had contacts with football clubs and was able to get hold of most of the football memorabilia.

The next day we all went to Walton-on-the-Naze where my brother's friend Paul was running a marathon and raising money for Chect.org.

28

THE IMPORTANT CHECK-UP

4TH MAY 2005

*M*aisy's check-up to see if the five sessions of chemotherapy had killed the tumours.

I felt so anxious that morning, considering what had happened on her last chemotherapy with the doctors having to stop the drug. I was convinced the doctors were going to give us bad news that day.

First, we saw Dr Kingston who checked Maisy's chest and weight and asked us about her health. She seemed fine and was much happier in herself, less clingy to me and was enjoying life. I explained to her that Maisy tilted her head a lot when she spoke to us or looked at us. She said she'd mention it to Mr Hungerford.

She was then given her eye drops, which she still hated. I would have to hold her down so the nurse could put the drops in her only eye. Even the offer of a sticker didn't stop her getting upset.

All the family were there that day, some of us around Maisy's bed, and some in the waiting room. I signed the usual consent forms, and Maisy was administered general anaesthetic as normal. All we could do now was wait and hope.

Eventually, later that afternoon, Sam and I were called in to see Mr Hungerford and Dr Kingston. I felt sick entering the room. The rest of our family were sat waiting anxiously for us to return.

It was good news. The best news! Mr Hungerford assured us the tumours were dead and he was happy with Maisy's progress. I wanted to kiss him!!! We couldn't thank him and Judith Kingston enough, they were just the best doctors and so good at their job.

We told the family the amazing news. I couldn't stop grinning and filling up with tears at the same time. Maisy really was amazing and a little fighter. We were all just so happy and relieved that the worst was over.

Mr Hungerford did explain that she would need check-ups every six weeks for the first two years, and then the appointments would slowly get further apart. Also, he said that the tumours could return anytime up to the age of five years old. He also said the reason Maisy tilts her head is that she simply sees much better in that position.

I got Maisy and gave Mr Hungerford and Dr Kingston a present. It was only something small, but I wanted to give them something to remember her by, and to say thank you. The presents were from a shop in Brentwood called Valdar, a small business that made decorated stones. The lady personalised the stones for me, and I thought that they could both use these as a paperweights in their offices.

So, although we left there in great spirits, we were still aware that Maisy was still prone to have this type of cancer return.

. . .

ON THE 6TH May I received a thank-you card in the post from Dr Kingston, thanking us for her gift. It was a nice surprise and I added it to Maisy's album that I was making.

My mum went tap dancing on Wednesday nights and had been at the same dance school for many years, forming a lovely circle of friends. One night when she returned home she gave me a present. A friend of my mum's, Rita Zetter, belonged to a sewing class, and her and two friends, Lyn Pointon and Maggie Griffin, had sewn a lovely patchwork blanket for Maisy, which I used a lot at my mum's house. I still have it and could never part with it. Rita also made Maisy a rag-doll and gave her some books.

Sam and I had already decided that as soon as Maisy was given the all-clear, we would return to Tenerife to continue our life as planned. So now this was all we could think about - getting back to some normality and to give Maisy a good life. We started looking at flights and told the family the plans. They were all disappointed, but I think they also understood that we needed to get away and continue what we'd started.

Before we booked our flights, my sister, Tina, announced that she had been arranging her wedding and she wanted Maisy to be a bridesmaid alongside her cousins. The wedding was very soon, so we went Debenhams at Lakeside to buy the girls their dresses and pretty shoes, and Tina also bought her wedding dress. It was really exciting; I think we all needed something to look forward to.

15TH MAY 2005

Sadly, I'm afraid to say I don't remember much of Tina and Kevin's wedding; I think I was still in my little world trying to process all we'd been through.

I do remember the venue, and that the girls looked lovely

in their bridesmaid dresses. Tina borrowed the tiara and wedding shoes that I had worn on my wedding, although I never did see either of them again!

I also remember our little Maisy walking down the aisle with her cousins. It was just so beautiful, and I was so proud of her as she smiled away. She just looked so happy. Who would have thought she had gone through what she had! Her hair was still quite fine and in a bob, and she was loving every minute of wearing her pretty dress and shoes, and being with her cousins. When she got to the end of the aisle the girls sat down, Sam picked Maisy up and sat her on his lap as we watched the ceremony.

29

TENERIFE

17TH MAY 2005

I think Sam and I needed to get away from England and hospitals. We just wanted to be a normal family. It was hard to leave my family as we had all been through so much, but at the same time I couldn't wait to escape England.

It was lovely to return to Tenerife and start afresh again. My sister, Paula, found an apartment we could stay in for a few weeks until we found somewhere else, and we managed to gradually get all our belongings out of storage and get our dog, Lola, back; it was really emotional seeing her. It felt like a holiday for a while, something we all desperately needed.

10TH AUG 2005

Three months later we returned to England for a check-up. It was lovely to see my family and best friends, and we stayed with my parents again. My mum came with me to the appointment at Buxton Ward and as always, we sat waiting.

When her name was called, she recognised the room. She hated the eye drops now. She was older and not as happy to sit and watch the bubbles, because she now knew what was coming next. She was crying while I held her head still for the doctor to place the mask on her face. Luckily it was only six or seven seconds before she was asleep. I felt like a horrible mum having to do that to her. I didn't cry but I was close.

Maisy got the all-clear, so that was fabulous news. Dr Kingston was happy with her growth and Mr Hungerford was happy with the dead tumours. Plus, we also managed to visit Primark and treat ourselves to some new clothes for the summer.

Hospital notes: *Check-up at Royal London Hospital. The enucleated right socket is free from recurrence with a good implant and prosthesis. Maisy was distressed when approached. Excellent prosthetic eye and no new tumours.*

Within a couple of months of our return to Tenerife the local newspaper got in contact with me as they wanted to write an up-to-date story in the local paper. I met up with Jacqueline Yuile, a writer, and gave her the full story, which she later published with a couple of lovely photos of Maisy.

5TH JULY

I found a headed letter from the Childhood Eye Cancer Trust in Maisy's album that I made for her. It was a thank you letter for a donation of £350 that was sent to them on behalf of the Brentwood Ladies Circus Moose International. The letter stated that they have also written a letter to Shelia Mobb thanking her and the ladies. Sheila was a lady I worked with years ago and I had kept in touch with her when I moved to Tenerife.

. . .

17TH OCTOBER

Maisy started at the Centro Infantile Peques, a Spanish nursery, three days a week from 9am to 2pm. I felt she needed to mix with other children and to have fun. The lady that owned the nursery was just so lovely and really looked after Maisy and she slowly started speaking the odd word of Spanish at home. She had to wear a uniform; a white t-shirt with Peques logo and a stripe down the side, plus navy-blue jogging bottoms with a matching stripe and red and yellow knee patches. Maisy loved going to this *guarderia* and was happy every time I dropped her off. She continued here until she started full time school.

We were enjoying life in Tenerife; Maisy absolutely loved the beach and swimming so most days we would be at the pool or the ocean. However, the sand would sometimes irritate Maisy's false eye so I would have to take it out and clean it.

I don't remember the first time I took her eye out myself. The doctors gave me this small piece of plastic, which we called the 'sucker'. It would stick to Maisy's false eye and then I would have to drag it down slowly and it would pop out. Putting it back in was always much harder as I was so careful not to hurt her and sometimes it would get stuck. She never enjoyed me taking her eye out or putting it back in, but she never cried.

I went to a bar one night to meet my sister, Paula, as she said there was a lady she knew that was of a similar age as me and had a baby girl the same age as Maisy. Paula thought it would be a good idea for us to meet. So, I did, and we got on really well. Her name was Lisa, and her little girl was called Eva. We all became good friends, and I loved Maisy having a friend. She and Eva would speak a mixture of English and Spanish to each other when they played. We're all still friends to this day.

. . .

9TH NOVEMBER

Hospital notes: *Royal London examination - seven months after completing chemotherapy, her general health remains good, and she had the first lot of her booster immunisations and is now awaiting a booster dose of the MMR vaccine.*

At this appointment I also mentioned that I was still not happy with her false eye as it still constantly moved. The nurse said she would speak to the team and see if they could recommend a different hospital for the false eye to be made.

Later that month I received a phone call to say that I would be getting a confirmation letter for an appointment with a hospital in Cambridgeshire for a new eye. I was very happy with this as I didn't want to return to Harold Wood Hospital.

DECEMBER 2005

Sam's parents decided to move to Tenerife to be near us all as they really missed Maisy, plus I was pregnant again, so they had another grandchild on the way. It was lovely having them around, and great for Maisy too.

17TH DECEMBER

We flew from Tenerife to Madrid to catch a connecting flight to Paris, all paid for from the money that Rita and Nicky raised at the charity night. Unfortunately, the afternoon we arrived; Maisy started feeling poorly. We had to call an ophthalmologist to the hotel room who said she had an infection in her false eye socket. We were given antibiotics, but Maisy was not in the best of moods whilst at Disneyland. She was just happy sitting in her pram wrapped up in a blanket and being walked around the park. We still had fun and went on loads of rides, and Tom and Paula treated her to some Disney souvenirs. I do also remember Tom buying me a green bracelet that I was looking at in the display cabinet. I still have this. It was our first time visiting Disneyland Paris and it was a holiday that we all needed, but just a shame that Maisy was not feeling great.

11TH JANUARY 2006

I was two months pregnant and feeling very healthy and well, with my baby due on July 17th, so Maisy, my bump and I, flew back to England.

At the Royal London Hospital, we spoke to Dr Kingston who told us that even though the chances of our new baby having the same change in the retinoblastoma gene as Maisy was low, they still need to check the new baby for the genetic change just in case.

She said this could be done by taking a blood sample from the umbilical cord when the baby is born and that we'd need to inform the midwives in Tenerife, and then let Dr Kingston know when baby was born and when bloods were on their way to the hospital.

Mr Hungerford was happy, no tumours, although Maisy had a slight cough. I assured them that she was fine before we flew and so we assumed she got it from the flight.

We received a letter the next day confirming our conversation with Dr Kingston, and enclosed was a covering letter, a bottle and a request form for the blood sample, as well as packaging for the sample to be posted back to the UK.

. . .

24TH JANUARY

Maisy had a false eye appointment at the new recommended hospital in Cambridge called Addenbrookes. Tina drove us there along with my mum. The oculist did the relevant moulding, took photos and said that he would be in contact with us in a few weeks.

7TH MARCH

We flew back to the UK for Maisy's new eye to be fitted, which looked okay at first, but by the time we got home, it had moved. I got upset as I didn't want Maisy to look different, and she'd also had lots of eye infections due to it not fitting correctly. I was always cleaning around her false eye, taking it out to clean it and buying eye drops to clear infections. I didn't understand why the eye could not be better and fit correctly.

The next day I phoned Mr Hungerford at the Royal London Hospital. He wasn't there but called me back later that day and said he would refer me to Moorfields Eye Hospital to see someone else.

The next day I took Maisy for a walk in her push chair to visit my friend, Clare Hayes. We'd known each other from school. It was nice to get out and get some fresh air. Clare made me a cup of tea while Maisy played on their rug in the living room. I remember talking to Clare's mum who had recently recovered from cancer, and she looked great.

We only stayed a few days in the UK and then flew back to Tenerife.

Memory from Clare: *Maisy was wearing a light brown woolly cardigan with flowers; Kay was holding Maisy and I remember looking at Kay and thinking how strong she was.*

(I still have this cardigan; it was one of my favourites for Maisy)

My mum told me a few days after returning to Tenerife that a letter had arrived for Maisy to see someone new at Moorfields Eye Hospital on the 1st of June 2006, so I booked flights for me and Maisy and we flew to Stansted on May 31st. Tina then drove us to the appointment the following day.

The doctor we saw was a very stern man, definitely not a 'children' person. The reason I say this is because Maisy was a bit irritable (and I don't blame her). I had her sat on my lap and I let her eat a pack of Quavers whilst he was looking at her eye. I didn't want my daughter to be upset; it can't be a great feeling having someone take your eye out! So, I was happy to let her eat crisps or anything she wanted just to make her content so she would sit there happily. But I could see that the doctor wasn't happy about her eating the crisps. He was quite rude and made no conversation with us other than briefly about her eye. However, I figured if Mr Hungerford had referred him then he must be good, so we just sat in silence whilst he took all the necessary photos and measurements that he needed, and then we left.

We returned two weeks later to get her new eye fitted and it looked great, so clever, and Maisy still never moaned about having her eye taken out. I always treated her afterwards with sweets or chocolate as she was so brave. the doctor didn't say much again apart from to advise us that she would need a new eye once a year.

10TH MAY

Hospital notes: *Check-up, weight 11.5kg, height 86.3, a year after chemo!*

Maisy was now two, and such a cutie. She loved dressing up in pretty tutus and dancing around the house to the Grease film soundtrack. She would wiggle her hips, singing and dancing to all the songs, though her favourite was *We Go Together*.

We were now living in a lovely bungalow in the resort of Island Village. It was quite small, but the garden was huge, and we had our own gardener called Paco. Maisy was always out in the garden either playing with Lola, running around, or playing on her slide. For some reason, she would call Sam, Sam, and not Dad. This went on for months, and drove Sam mad, but it made me laugh every time!

Back in Tenerife, I organised a charity afternoon at a local restaurant, The Carvery, where Sam, my sister Paula and I worked. We made cakes and organised a raffle and raised £328. Maisy would always be with me helping to hand out the cakes and helping with the raffle. Everyone just loved her and because we all worked there everyone knew Maisy.

I was working in an office next to the swimming pool and the lifeguard, Juan, was so good with Maisy. In fact he was great with any kids that were on holiday or lived on the resort. Now and then he would come into the office and take Maisy for a walk, sharing his home-made biscuits, which were lovely. If the resort was quiet, he would happily take her for a swim. Fortunately, she loved the water and learnt to swim at the age of two-and-a-half.

Maisy had also started ballet dancing at a local English-run dance school, Ritmania, owned by Carla and Emma. They were lovely and we soon became good friends. Dancing runs in our family so it was only natural for Maisy to start. She was two and half and loved her first class. I remember watching her through the window of the reception area. I have a lovely video of Maisy dancing with Carla learning good toes and naughty toes. She was wearing pink shorts, a white t-shirt, ballet shoes and a pink headband. with her hair in plaits. Carla had Maisy dancing to Bippety Boppety Boo and skipping across the room. She was the youngest in the class and could never say the word 'ballet', pronouncing it 'baylet' instead.

1ST JUNE

Hospital notes: *Eye inflamed and red, and with yellow discharge. Mould taken, but mother may not be able to return to the UK as she is due a baby. Suggested to buy chloramphenicol eye drops*

30

HARRY WAS BORN!

30TH JULY 2006

*D*ue to Maisy being born with Retinoblastoma, when I gave birth, blood would need to be taken from the placenta and sent to the UK as soon as possible for the doctors to test.

Maisy was a great big sister although she kept saying she was his brother. I have her saying this on video over and over again. She really didn't understand that he was a brother, and she was a sister. They really did have the best life! Tenerife was a lovely, relaxed place to live, and they were close to my sister and their Uncle Tom who would help look after them at weekends. Plus, they had their big cousins Maxi and Jimmi to play with on the beach. They were happy kids.

We had to wait to hear from the hospital to make sure Harry had not inherited the same gene, but I don't remember worrying too much whilst we waited. I was quite confident that he didn't have it… surely not again!

10TH SEPTEMBER 2006

The moment of truth. My mum received a letter

addressed to Sam and me. I asked her to open it and was desperately happy to hear it was good news. Harry was clear and didn't need to have any check-ups.

Maisy loved her little brother Harry, she always wanted to cuddle him, and now and then she would want Harry to sit on her lap so she could hold him. She also loved bath time with Harry. and helping me feed him his milk and changing his nappy.

31

CHECK-UPS

2006

*M*y mum took a couple of days off work as we were flying to the UK.

These cancer check appointments were always a worry when Maisy would go into theatre alone and all we could do was sit and wait. However, Mr Hungerford and Dr Kingston were still happy with Maisy's progress and reported no new tumours. Caroline, the play specialist, was still there so I had a catch-up while me and Mum drank lots of tea.

Hospital notes: *Maisy enjoying nursery school, she can drink from a cup and full potty trained. Maisy is very cooperative and appears to be growing satisfactorily. Notes also stated that she had measles in June and was admitted with breathing problems, antibiotics given, and full recovery made. As Maisy has a scar at the site of the previously treated tumour involving the macula in her left eye, her central vision is not going to be normal. We will be able to assess this as she gets older. All being well on her next check-up in 4 months we can then extend it to 6 months appointments.*

We also went to have another new eye made for Maisy; it was beginning to look too small for her eye socket and she was overdue a new eye. Whilst the doctor applied the custard to Maisy's eye, I noticed he was getting agitated as Maisy wouldn't listen to what he wanted her to do. He really wasn't a people person, and again I found him very rude. But he made good false eyes, so I just kept quiet.

I stayed in the UK until Maisy's eye was made. Before the fitting, Maisy and I were sat in a room at Moorfields with only a curtain between us and the next patient who was waiting to be seen. I could hear this same oculist talking to a young girl on the other side. The young girl's mum was explaining that she wasn't happy with her daughter's eye, and she was being bullied at school for looking different. He didn't make the girl feel confident at all, and just said he said it was the best he could do. I was welling up hearing what he was saying to her, he really was not good with children. I could hear the girl getting upset and yet he never said a nice word to her, or try to give her some confidence, or to say that he would do his best next time to make the eye better. I felt really sad for the young girl as it must have really knocked her confidence.

Maisy had her new eye fitted and it looked amazing. The colours were perfect and when she looked at you straight ahead you'd never have known it was a false eye.

I remember walking back through the waiting room and there was a young girl about 13 years old sitting with her mum. I can only assume it was the young girl I had overheard. For the rest of the day, I kept thinking about that young girl and how unhappy she was. I phoned the hospital and complained about this particular oculist and told them what I'd heard, and I asked if I could have a different oculist next time I visited. There was no way I was going to let Maisy be treated the same as he'd treated that young girl.

. . .

17TH JANUARY 2007

Hospital notes: *No new tumours, no signs of pain, no nausea or vomiting, awake and eyes open at 15.50.*

She is a delightful, nearly 3-year-old girl, still gets discharge from the false eye. However, she is now more cooperative and lets her mother take out the prosthetic eye to clean it. She was very cooperative and looks well.

Maisy having problems at nursery seeing pictures from a distance or on blackboard, but okay with print near her when reading. No new tumours have developed, Maisy will be three at the end of this month and we will see her again in six months' time.

32

FUNDRAISERS

27TH FEBRUARY 2007

*W*e organised a family fun run where each person had to run 24 miles in their own time, but on a chosen date all the runners had to run the last mile together starting from The Carvery restaurant and running around the area. The runners were Paula, Jimmi, Maxi, Helen, Jake, Gavin, Lena and Lisa. Between them they raised £1990 in sponsorship money.

We also held a raffle where many local businesses donated some great prizes such as massage vouchers, boat trips, dance classes and more. I didn't do the run as I was looking after the kids.

Gavin and Sarah from The Carvery raised £515 between them in donations.

23RD MARCH 2007

Next up was the Big Blue and White Charity Event. Dress code was formal, blue and/or white, and it started at 6.30pm with a welcome cocktail, followed by a fabulous buffet and entertainment throughout the evening.

Through my job I was lucky enough to meet a lot of people that sold excursions or entertained at different bars and restaurants on the island. I had managed to ask many singers from the island to kindly give their services for free and sing for us. We had Dion, Mystic Girls, and Michaela as Tina Turner, plus the Stardust Show and more.

An auction and a raffle were also held. Proceeds from these was to help us with flights back to and from the UK. My sister made some great tickets and posters to help advertise the event and we sold many tickets. Maisy was now 3 years old and loved helping at the event. She wore white leggings and a blue dress with white pumps.

The auction prizes were:

- 1 dive for 1 person; Dave at Black Cove Divers
- Parascending for 1 person; Las Vistas Beach
- 3-day car hire Panda; Amarilla Cars
- Weekend getaway for 2, including 2 days, 2 nights in a hillside retreat in La Escalona, in a lovely countryside studio; The Paper
- Weekend for 2 in Club La Paz, Puerto de la Cruz; Crown Resorts Corporation

Raffle prizes included:

- Hair and makeup: Blueberry Bobs
- Teddy: Little Treasures
- Basket of wine: Magic Moments
- Blow Dry: Blue Rain
- Massage and pedicure: Vicky
- 1-month free membership for 1 person; Metropolis gym x 2
- 1 free dance class: Ritmania Escuela de Baile
- Carvery meal for 2: The Carvery

- Eporex vouchers: Eporex Centre
- 2 cocktails: Harley's Restaurant
- Golf lesson for 1 person: Javier Toll. Amarillo Golf
- Basket of body shop products: Magic Moments
- Carvery meal for 2: The Carvery restaurant
- 30 minutes tanning session: The Tanning Centre
- 2 games of bowling: Harley's super bowl
- Photography Voucher: New world photography

Balloon Warehouse decorated the event free with blue and white balloons.

It was such a fab night; we raised 560 euros in ticket sales and 1000 euros on the raffle.

A journalist from the local paper, *The Paper*, kindly wrote an article of thanks to everyone that sang, helped out, attended and helped raise money.

By now, Maisy was a chatty kid and very bossy. She loved music and still loved to dance especially to the film, *Grease*. She would watch it on TV and rewind the same song over and over again. I have a memory of her dancing and wiggling her bum wearing knickers, pink plastic heels, and a satin 'Pink Ladies' jacket made by the mum of my best friend, Toni. Maisy loved it, and we actually still have it.

I'm not sure when this was exactly, but it's a memory I have; Sam, Maisy, Paula, Tom, Maxi, Jimmi and I had been to our local carvery restaurant at Island Village for a roast dinner. I remember standing outside The Carvery on the steps chatting to Tom while the kids were all running around at the top area outside the restaurant. Out of the blue, Tom said that I was not the same person I used to be. He added that Maxi and Jimmi had both noticed it too.

I was shocked that someone had actually said it to me, especially Tom. But I also knew I was not the same person. 'How can I be after what I have been through? I replied.

'I know I know,' he said in his Scottish accent.

I wasn't upset with Tom saying that to me, but I was upset that I had changed. I wasn't as happy as I was even though I loved my life in Tenerife. I knew I was not that person anymore.

26TH MARCH

Another charity afternoon, playing killer pool, and I had a jar on my desk at work for donations. We also did a 4-mile fun run from Island Village to San Eugenio and back to The Carvery restaurant. Sam returned first.

16TH MAY

Back to business at the day clinic in St Bartholomew's Hospital where another consent form was signed while we waited to see Mr Hungerford and Dr Kingston. Thankfully all was good news.

We were so lucky that no new tumours grew during this time. I couldn't wait for Maisy to be five years old so I wouldn't have this worry at each appointment.

Hospital notes: *The right eye is entirely healthy and is free from recurrence. There are no new tumours in the left eye and the old ones are all inactive.*

26TH MAY

Ritmania dance school performed a show at Pleasure Island in Las Americas, during which, they raised £400 for Retinoblastoma. I always loved watching Maisy dance as she loved it and was so good at it; I just loved seeing her happy and being a normal child.

30TH MAY

Dia De La Canarias (Canary Islands Day) was one of my favourite fiestas in Tenerife. I'd bought Maisy a typical, green and white Canarian outfit to wear. Paula, Maisy and I went to visit Maxi and Jimmi at their school as they were having a party. Maisy looked so cute, I have a lovely photo of Maisy and Maxi dressed up in their Canarian outfits.

Not long after, she had her last day at Peques Guarderia as summer holidays in Tenerife started in June. It was emotional on her last day. I was allowed to go in and watch her sing and dance and she was given a gift from her teachers. She gave them all a hug and they wished her well in her new school.

33

MORE CHECK-UPS

28TH JUNE 2007

*A*ppointment with Moorfields Eye Hospital at 12.30pm as Maisy was a due a new eye. This time we saw a different oculist named Dr Carpenter. He was lovely and chatty, and I really liked him. He did the same moulding and photos of Maisy and said the eye would be ready in a few weeks.

It was a quick visit to the UK but lovely to spend time with my family.

3RD AUGUST 2007

Maisy, Harry and I flew back for Maisy's new eye. We stayed for a week as it was the English school holidays, so we had some days to spend with my sister, Tina, and her kids. Maisy got her new eye, which was amazing, and we were moved to a new building around the back of Moorfields. It was a lot nicer and newer and included a coffee shop. Maisy said her new eye was comfortable, so we left happy, hand in hand.

. . .

3RD September

Maisy started at big Spanish school in Adeje called Casco. Children started full-time school at the age of three back then. The school didn't have a uniform; she could wear what she wanted, normally shorts and a t-shirt, and trainers or pumps. She was little, but it was normal for her to start at 8.30am and finish at 3pm, five days a week. I really think it was good for her, her Spanish was coming along well, and she enjoyed it.

During her school years in Tenerife no children ever asked Maisy about her eye, they just accepted her, and there was no bullying, which made school much more enjoyable.

The staff were also lovely. She still talks about a teacher, Juan Domingo, who she adored. The teachers loved their jobs and most importantly loved the kids. Every morning the maintenance man who opened the school gates would high five the kids or give them a cuddle. Same as Juan Domingo, he always cuddled the kids. I was really happy with her time at this school.

14TH NOVEMBER

Maisy, Harry and I flew back to UK, and fortunately, they were both good kids, so the flight was not stressful on my own. I loved this time of year when it was chilly, and we got to go to Romford to do Christmas shopping. Even though we only needed a small case with us I paid extra for a bigger case so I could buy Maisy and Harry's presents, which meant that any spare time was spent Christmas shopping with my mum or Tina.

16TH NOVEMBER

I have a photo of Maisy looking happy during a cancer

check-up, sitting crossed legged on the hospital bed wearing bright coloured striped tights with a yellow dress and a grey hoodie covered in stars. She was also wearing a big sticker that said 'I had my drops'.

Maisy was now growing out of the risk period, but they still needed to see her again in six months, and it was possible that they would be able to see her awake in the outpatients rather than under anaesthetic. When Mr Hungerford explained this, it was such a relief as we would no longer have to tell her she couldn't eat until she came back from theatre. Plus, she wouldn't have to go under anaesthetic, she could be awake with me in the room beside her.

> **Hospital notes:** *Good health but has several warts on her chest, now in reception class at school, having problems with seeing the blackboard or wall at school, but okay with bigger print.*

She was also able to have a visual assessment now that she was older, and the orthoptist advised that she would possibly need a low vision aid to facilitate her schoolwork.

34

MORE FUNDRAISERS AND CHECK-UPS

2008

2 9th February 2008

We'd organised a charity ball at La Fortaleza del Mar, a local restaurant in Puerto Colon, a pretty place overlooking the sea. Sadly, at the time of writing, it's no longer there, the premises now occupied by Kaluna Beach Club.

Paula designed and printed off the tickets and between family and friends we tried to sell as many tickets as we could. The evening included champagne cocktail on arrival and a three-course meal consisting of a selection of starters, carvery and dessert. Again, we had many singers and dancers to entertain us throughout the evening, as well as a raffle and auction.

Maisy and her dance group from Ritmania performed for everybody; they all wore tutus and flower headbands. It was so lovely, and she looked so cute doing what she loved.

This year I had written to *Real People Magazine* to see if they would like to write a story about Maisy. I didn't think they would get in touch, but to my surprise they did. We did the interview over the phone, and I sent them many photos of Maisy and all of us together. In return they paid me £250 which was still needed to help with flight money. I was still returning to the UK at least 3 or 4 times a year, and although flights back then were cheaper compared to now, it was still a lot of money to keep paying out, so any help was appreciated. Our families would help as and when they could, plus Sam and I were both working.

4TH MAY

It had been three years since Maisy had finished her chemotherapy, and we were sat waiting at Royal London Hospital before she went under anaesthetic. Although on our last check-up we were told that she may not have to go under anaesthetic anymore, the letter we received stated she did.

She was so well behaved and just let the nurses do their checks on her without any moaning or crying, although she still hated having the eye drops. I was never able to relax until she was out and back in my arms for a cuddle and felt well enough to eat.

Then came the news I'd been waiting for. Mr Hungerford called me into a room alone while Mum stayed with Maisy. He sat me down and told me that all the tumours were still dead, and that Maisy doesn't need any further examinations under anaesthetic, and he'd arranged to see her in the outpatient clinic in six months' time. Yay, finally!

Hospital notes: *Her false eye was the best eye so far; mum is still saying that Maisy struggles at school; I am forwarding details to get her registered as partially blind.*

13TH JUNE

I organised a sponsored walk starting at Coral Mar Square and walking to *Montaña Amarilla* (Yellow Mountain). There were a lot of us that day - Katja, Jayne, Helen, Clare and Paula to name a few. We all wore comfy clothes and rucksacks stocked with water as it was a hot day. I remember it being a lovely walk along the beach and when we reached the mountain the views were amazing. I have a few sponsor forms from that day that I had kept in Maisy's album and I'm sure we raised a few hundred euros.

'Life Returning to Normal' was the headline in another article written by Jacqui Yuile for the local paper. We had been doing the odd small charity event to raise money, but I now wanted to do something bigger. Jacqui had previously written about our lives and kindly advertised the next event too.

The article stated that Maisy now had a baby brother, and due to Maisy being born with Retinoblastoma we were told that when I gave birth, blood would need to be taken from the placenta and sent to the UK as soon as possible for the doctors to test it. It recalled how we had to wait seven weeks to get the results but that they were all clear. She also wrote brief details of the event, including my phone number if any wished to purchase a ticket for the night.

15TH JUNE

We always managed to get lost in the Royal London Hospital, and this time was no exception. We eventually found the room we were supposed to attend and, after having her eye drops and being checked by the specialist, Maisy was pronounced well and healthy. It was always a relief. We left there and walked to find some lunch as a treat, then got the train back to Nana Hazel's.

. . .

20TH JUNE

Maisy's dance school were always willing to help me with any charity event I organised. This time we'd arranged for Ritmania to dance at the Fortaleza del Mar restaurant to raise money for the Eye Cancer Trust. While the ticket money went to the dance school, proceeds from the raffle were sent by cheque to chect.org. This event was advertised in the local paper too. The girls danced in ribbons, and black, all-in-one leotards; they all looked so cute and danced wonderfully.

8TH JULY

Another appointment for a new eye to be made. Again, we had the same oculist as last time, Dr Carpenter. We were much more comfortable with him. He did the necessary photos and measurements, and polished Maisy's false eye then told us that he'd be in touch when the eye was ready.

25TH JULY

Maisy still didn't really understand what was happening when we went to Moorfields Eye Hospital, but she never moaned about getting a new eye. We were so happy with it and the colour was amazing, it fitted so well.

14TH AUGUST

Mum came with me to Maisy's cancer check-up and we had our usual catch-up with Caroline, the play specialist. Another consent form was signed by me, and then all we could do was wait.

Our wait was well worth it though. It was all good news as Mr Hungerford's team were happy with her, and naturally so were we. I always left that hospital with a smile. Until next time!

12TH NOVEMBER

Her hair was getting longer and thicker now, and she had wavy hair and a fringe.

I explained to Dr Kingston that Maisy had started to squint slightly and still moved her head to the side when she talked to me. She checked Maisy's chest, her height and weight, and told me she seemed well.

When it was our turn to see Mr Hungerford, he confirmed the good news that he was pleased with her progress and confirmed that Maisy's tumour was on the centre of her pupil which would explain why she tilts her head when looking at me to talk.

Hospital notes: *She was able to cooperate sufficiently to have her left ocular fundus examined awake and I am pleased to say no new tumours. Parents fit and well, brother has asthma. Mum also asked if Maisy is now registered as partially sighted, I advised her she is and will send her confirmation of the certificate.*

We were now on yearly appointments for the Royal London Hospital, and now that she was over five, we could be transferred to the new centre at Royal London.

35

ANOTHER YEAR

2009

*2*0th April 2009

Paula made charity run sponsor forms for me with a photo of Maisy in a silver dress.

None of the ladies that took part were runners, but we had to cover 5 miles in our own time, then the last mile altogether on this date, starting from Hooters. There was me, Sam, Gary and Helen and a few others that joined us that day.

> **Memory from friend Helen;** *I remember this day. There were quite a lot of people. I had only recently become friends with Kay, and I met all her family there that day.*

After the run we walked to The Carvery in Island Village and had a party. I raised 700 euros in sponsorship money. I remember buying some toys for Great Ormond Street and Royal London hospital with the proceeds of this.

22ND MAY

Maisy was now 5 years old and today was her first appointment at the outpatient clinic at St. Bart's Hospital to have an examination without being put under anaesthetic. It was such a relief that I didn't have to put her through this anymore, and nor did I have to sign another consent form. Plus, I was able to go in with her and stay with her through the whole check-up. She was so good, just sat on my lap as they popped her false eye out and had a good look inside with their lights. She continued to sit while they took photos of her eye; I was proud that she was so good and happy to sit there.

Hospital notes: *Prosthetic falls out when she sneezes so have brought new eye appointment forward.*

Now that Maisy was over the age of five, Retinoblastoma was not likely to return. However, she was now prone to skin cancer. I was advised by Dr Kingston to always keep an eye on any moles or lumps appearing on Maisy's body.

26TH MAY

The oculist at Moorfields asked how Maisy has been and asked her if she is enjoying school. Then he checked her over and agreed she needed a new eye made. As usual he took her false eye into another room and polished it for her. We weren't in there long and then we got the train straight back to Nana Hazel's house.

2ND JUNE

The Black and White charity night at James Brasserie in Tenerife included a champagne cocktail on arrival followed by a carvery roast dinner. Everyone had to wear black and or white. I'd organised singers again, and this time we had the lovely Jo, Elaine Alexander Morris, and sisters Karen Gorse and Lucinda Jones. We also had Maisy's dance teachers, Emma and Carla, there for support too.

Maisy gave the best performance of the night. I'd explained to her that I was organising a charity night and asked her if she would perform for us. Together we agreed on a song by Eminem and Rhianna, Love the Way You Lie, because it was both slow and fast. Maisy choreographed a slow dance, along with some hip hop moves too. She wore a pink crop top, a white tutu and went barefoot. She was just amazing; there wasn't a dry eye in the house that night.

26ᵀᴴ JUNE

We flew back to the UK to have Maisy's new eye fitted. By now I'd lost count of how many eyes we had at home. Her new eye was fitted, and we left the hospital all happy and smiling then walked back to Liverpool Street to get the train to Harold Wood.

I HAVE a letter dated 30th July 2010 from Sue Soloman, president of San Miguel De Abona De Lions in Costa del Silencio in Tenerife. They had held a BBQ fundraiser afternoon and sent us a cheque for 236 Euros. The letter also stated that they would like to help us in the future with flights and any medical help. It was so nice that people wanted to help; Maisy was just loved so much. I did contact them and as promised they helped us with flights that we needed for her next appointment in the UK, so once more I'd like to say thank you so much.

· · ·

TOWARDS THE END of the year, we heard that Mr Hungerford was retiring from the NHS and only taking private appointments. We were sad to hear this, but thankfully Maisy was over the worst and Mr Hungerford had trained a great team at Royal London to take over from him.

It was around this time that Maisy started asking questions about her eye. Luckily, I had made the album for Maisy and had been adding photos and notes over the years. She didn't understand the word cancer, but she knew she had a poorly eye. I remember her asking me why Harry didn't have a poorly eye. It was quite sad hearing this, and Maisy was slightly annoyed whilst asking me. But within five minutes she was off playing outside, completely unaffected by what she had asked me, or my answer. For a couple of days, I was a lot quieter, pondering over how a 5-year-old deals with that.

3RD DECEMBER

Maisy's brother, George was born!!

We had to do the same again, send bloods back to UK to be checked, and after weeks of waiting, George got the all clear too. Maisy now had two little brothers to annoy her.

36

MOVING ON

2010

3 1st January 2010 - Maisy's birthday
Maisy's hair was so lovely and long now and getting so thick. She had a lovely morning opening presents. She was really into Hannah Montana, and I brought her some white, patent leather Hannah Montana boots and a bright pink top. She loved those boots and would wear them everywhere, even to walk Lola our dog.

10TH MAY

We arrived at Moorfields Eye Hospital and were greeted by a different oculist called Peter who was lovely and chatty. Maisy immediately took a liking to him and wasn't at all shy as he asked her about school and her hobbies. He took her false eye out with a small plastic sucker and had a look at her good eye, which by now had completely changed colour. On the false eye the specialist had painted coloured dots, so we knew which way her eye was supposed to go in when we had to put it back after cleaning it.

Peter said he would send a letter when the eye was ready to be fitted.

30TH JUNE

New eye made

Another new eye by Peter, the colour and detail were so good that you could see the blood vessels that he'd painted on the eye.

17TH SEPTEMBER

Another new eye fitting

Hospital notes: *Eye needs more colours, green and slightly darker.*

In October that year I organised a walk to climb *Montaña Roja* in El Medano. We all met at where the baby class was in Coral Mar Square and started our hike along the beach. It was a lovely walk, and one that I'd wanted to do since living in Tenerife. We stopped at a bar on the way back to rest our legs and have an alcoholic drink or two! With the proceeds, I planned to buy some craft materials for the Royal London Hospital.

10TH NOVEMBER

We returned to the UK to collect Maisy's new eye which was great! The colour looked exactly the same as her left eye. Maisy was now six and still happy to let them take out her false eye and sit waiting in the chair for her eye to be polished.

Tina organised an early Christmas dinner whilst we were

there, so I went shopping for table crackers and presents for everybody. Tina and Kevin made a lovely roast dinner with all the trimmings, and we all wore Christmas jumpers and t-shirts. Tina bought Maisy a pink ballet dress for Christmas, which she loved. We had a great day, eating, chatting and playing games with the kids.

TIME FLIES

2011

*2*0th January 2011

Hospital notes (from a check-up with Mr Hungerford's Team): *I saw Maisy today as her mother had noticed a white fleck in her left eye. All the tumours seem to be inert and no activity. Will see her in 12 months' time.*

4TH MARCH

Both Maisy and Harry were dressed up and walking the streets of Adeje with Casco school to celebrate the Carnival. It was a lovely celebration, and all the pupils and teachers were involved. They played loud music, and everyone was happy dressed in their costumes. I loved celebrating Carnival in Tenerife.

20TH MARCH

I remember I'd done this *Barranco del Infierno* (Hell's Ravine) walk with Tina when I was about 15 years old. I was looking forward to this day as I remember it being a nice walk. I met Paula, Katja, Clare and many others at Otelo Restaurant car park from where we set off on what was a lovely, but slightly dangerous, walk, chatting all the way to the small waterfall that marked the end. I planned to buy some toys for the hospital with the proceeds collected from everyone that day.

3ᴿᴰ JULY

Another charity event at The Carvery, this time with a pink and black theme. I have no notes of this but found some photos to remind me. I wore a pink dress and Maisy was in a pink glittery skirt, a pink crop top, and had a pink bow in her hair. Harry looked very smart in jeans, pink t-shirt and a black waistcoat.

Hollie and Eddie Hastings were the comperes and singers for the night. Eddie wore a bright pink, silk suit, and Hollie was wearing a lovely pink dress. I also had a few other singers who gave their time for free.

One of the evening acts that I particularly remember was the lovely Saphryn Townsend who was dressed like Rhianna. Her costume was fab, and Rhianna was huge at the time. Maisy loved her. We were all up dancing when she sang. Karen Gorse and Lucinda also sang, as did Ash and Vinnie Love, and Michelle Almgill. It was a brilliant night.

6ᵀᴴ AUGUST

Maisy's dance school were performing to a full crowd of drinkers and diners for a charity event. Maisy and the girls from Ritmania were all excited and they performed beautifully.

The compere that day was Ollie Cusack who called me over to him and told me he knew about Maisy. He'd recently lost sight in his eye and therefore could relate to Maisy. We had a good chat, and I remember him telling Maisy how good she was at dancing.

Memory from Ollie Cusack: *Maisy gave me the biggest cuddle ever and told me that everything was going to be okay. She brought tears to my eyes. I will never forget that day.*

Maisy continued to perform with Ritmania in Los Cristianos in many dance shows, town fiestas and in their own summer dance spectacular too. I would always get emotional watching her, just grateful she was here, enjoying what she loved doing.

10ᵀᴴ NOVEMBER

Moorfields Eye Hospital

The next time we flew back to Moorfields Eye Hospital her eyes were a completely different colour again. Peter advised the eye would be ready in a few weeks.

I returned to the UK where the kids spent lots of days playing with their cousins. Maisy had the new eye fitted which was amazing. I was grateful that we had finally found a good oculist. Peter always had time to chat and ask how Maisy was doing. He would always re-assure her that he would make a better eye that would be very similar to her good eye.

I still enjoyed coming back to the UK to see my family and to go shopping for clothes; there were many more clothes shops in England than in Tenerife. We'd also make sure we spent time at my sisters too, so the kids could see each other. It was always sad to return to Tenerife in some ways, but the kids loved their life there, and I did too.

38
ANOTHER YEAR OLDER

2012

th February 2012

Hospital notes: *Maisy is still not able to take her eye out and replace it on her own, today we will carry out some teaching to try and build Maisy's confidence.*

I felt that the nurse was very abrupt with me that day. I remember she seemed concerned that I wasn't encouraging Maisy enough to take her own eye out and replace it. I told the nurse that Maisy was still very young and if she was happy with me taking her eye out for her then I would continue to do so until she felt ready. The nurse still seemed insistent that Maisy should learn how to do this herself, but I repeated that I wouldn't be pushing her. I could understand if she was a teenager, then maybe she should be wanting to take the eye out herself. But I felt she wasn't ready; she was still so tiny to me.

At the hospital we were advised by Caroline that we were entitled to a wish from the Make a Wish Foundation. I received an email from her a few days later explaining that because we lived in Spain, we had to request a wish from the Spanish Make a Wish organisation. Caroline said that she'd contacted them in Spain, and someone would get in contact with me soon. Maisy gave Caroline a huge stack of craft materials that we had bought with the money raised.

A couple of weeks later a lady from Make a Wish phoned me and asked me all about Maisy and what wish I thought she would like. We discussed options, but Maisy loved princesses and I knew that she would love Disneyland, especially as the first time we visited she was very young and too poorly to enjoy it. Make a Wish said they would send me the details once they had planned our trip.

A lady from Make a Wish phoned me a couple of weeks later to discuss dates of when we would like to go to Disneyland Paris. She said she would be finalising the details and would send us confirmation in the post. The lady was nice and sounded really excited about our trip to Disneyland. So was I!

20TH NOVEMBER

Her new eye was amazing! Peter is so good with Maisy, making sure she feels okay and is happy before she leaves the hospital.

29TH NOVEMBER

We received a small parcel from Make a Wish addressed to Maisy, Harry, and George with the full itinerary for our holiday to Paris. We would be flying with Iberia at 7.20am and would arrive in Madrid at 11.10am. From there, we were to catch another plane at 14.10 to Paris.

Everything was arranged; we flew to Madrid to catch our

connecting flight to Paris. From there, we travelled by coach to our final destination.

We stayed at the Newport Bay Hotel, and from the moment we checked in, we were well looked after. Maisy and the boys were given vouchers to spend in the hotel shop, plus an Aladdin-themed lanyard. The receptionist informed us that we had to show the lanyard on every ride to receive VIP treatment. Sam and I then took the kids straight into the shop to spend their vouchers. While Maisy had more vouchers than the boys, Harry was more than happy that he could pick something for free. Both boys opted for a Buzz Lightyear cup with a straw, and Maisy selected a Tinkerbell cup with a straw and a princess notepad.

Afterwards, we headed to our room to drop off our luggage and immediately ventured out to the park. The lack of queues for us was a real bonus, and we made it our mission to meet as many characters as we could while exploring the park. Maisy particularly loved the 'A Small World' ride and the teacups.

We had a lovely meal in the evening which was all booked and paid for. On our second day we were told to be in a certain area at a certain time. Sam and I didn't know where we were going either, so it was a surprise for us all.

A man took us into a small room and asked Maisy who her favourite princess was, and if she'd enjoyed Paris so far. Then the door opened, and Snow White, Jasmine and Belle entered the room. Harry was so shy and hid behind my leg while I was holding George on my hip. They asked Maisy questions, and we took photos with them until they said goodbye.

Just to see Maisy's face was amazing, she was so happy and was having the best time, and so were the boys. They loved the pretend snow that was blowing out from the shops on the main street. We had lots of photos with the characters in the hotel. The kids really enjoyed all the rides too, and the street shows were fabulous. We all had a lovely time.

DECEMBER 2012

Maisy's dance school participated in the Islavision Dance Competition to compete against other dance schools. This was the Canary Islands' equivalent to Britain's Got Talent but for dance groups only.

The kids were getting nervous as I remember them waiting around for a while until it was their turn to perform. All the girls looked so cute with long hair and pig tails, and wore their pyjamas for the dance as it fitted in with the song.

Finally, the announcement was made, 'Ritmania school of Dance'! They danced so well! We were all so proud of them... and then they only went and won! We were all so overwhelmed and proud of them all and they got a lovely big trophy. On the way home in the coach, it was buzzing, and Carla and Emma were unbelievably proud that day. You can find the video on YouTube by searching for 'Islavision Ritmania'.

39

TIME MARCHES ON

2013

5th March
    Back in UK for a cancer check-up.

Hospital notes: *Maisy seems to be enjoying school and dancing, she continues to have no problems with her tumours.*

7th March
Maisy was a massive fan of Justin Bieber. She loved him, and I'd bought tickets to see him at the 02 Arena back in London for a Christmas present. I remember she wore blue denim shorts and a pink t-shirt with 'I love Bieber' written on it. When we talk about that night now, she still remembers how excited she was... and she's still a Bieber fan!

5TH NOVEMBER
    Moorfields Eye Hospital. I always timed these appointments near Christmas so I could do some Christmas shopping. The kids loved a plane trip to see their cousins, but not so keen on the cold weather. It was always a shock to us

all, but I loved having to wrap up in big coats, scarves and gloves.

We got the train with my mum to Moorfields for her eye fitting, then got the train to Liverpool Street where we popped into WHSmith to buy some goodies for the train journey back to Harold Wood.

The next day we went to Romford, where I managed to buy a few Christmas presents, and later that night, grandad Colin had the kids while Tina, my mum and I went to Lakeside to do some more shopping.

7ᵀᴴ NOVEMBER

We received a letter from Learning Support Service about Maisy's visual assessment:

Maisy maybe be unaware that people or objects are on her right side, this can be especially hazardous in unfamiliar surroundings.

She may experience difficulty with materials and gestures presented on her right side, and mobility in unfamiliar surroundings.

Test for colour vision: Maisy experienced some difficulties in seeing some of the colour images, she may have a weakness in distinguishing between red/and or green.

Maisy has difficulty judging distances and depth.

She may sometimes not recognise steps, kerbs unless clearly marked.

Changes in floor surfaces, I.E from carpet to lino may be mistaken for different levels.

She may show difficulties with activities including pouring liquid, threading and cutting.

Ball games may be more difficult with a child with monocular vision.

Memory from Paula: *Maisy had always been so strong throughout everything and not letting it bother her as she grew up over here. She was a little superstar in The Carvery restaurant, especially when we had charity events. She was always singing and dancing and putting on shows for everyone. All the Spanish staff on the resort where we held the events absolutely loved her too.*

We returned to the UK a few days after George's fourth birthday. We'd had a small party at nana Hazel's house with a cake and balloons, and all the kids played together. It was so lovely seeing them all together, and it did make me sad that I was taking them away from their cousins and they wouldn't be seeing them again for another few months.

Before we left, Maisy got her new eye fitted. It was an early appointment so afterwards we all went to the science museum, which the kids loved.

40

YEAR OF THE RETURN

2014

*1*st March 2014

Maisy was now nine years old. She had a cancer check-up and they took photos of her eye. It was very interesting to see photos of the tumours on the screen, but I could see Maisy felt uncomfortable as they stood so close to her, almost face-to-face to shine a torch in her left eye. The doctor then removed her false eye and checked her socket to make sure there were no infections. The team said this was also a new way of checking the tumours.

6ᵀᴴ May

We'd noticed that only a few months after having her new eye fitted that already it looked too small as she was obviously growing a lot quicker. Peter, the oculist, had already advised me that she might need a new eye every six months. He agreed the eye was too small and the colour was also slightly different; she had piercing blue eyes when she was born and now, they were beginning to turn green. He said he would do his best to get the eye made as quickly as possible.

9ᵀᴴ JUNE

Maisy and I were there for about three hours, but we didn't mind as the eye specialist at the Royal London Hospital told us that the tumours were still dead. The doctor did advise us though that because Maisy had quite a lot of moles that they would like to get her checked every six months or yearly by our local doctor. She was referred to Queens's Hospital in Romford, and an appointment was set for a few months' time.

The next day Maisy had her new eye appointment, so Maisy and I got the train to Liverpool Street and then walked the 20 minutes to Moorfields Eye Hospital. I bought a coffee from the small, hospital coffee shop and then waited to be seen. We had never waited more than five minutes for any of our appointments. The door opened and Peter approached us with a smile on his face as always. We followed him into his room, and he had a catch-up with Maisy and asked her how her eye had been. She told him that she still got the odd eye infection but otherwise the eye was comfortable.

WE MOVED BACK to the UK in August 2014. I loved Tenerife and miss it most days, but I felt I needed to return to the UK. It was partly for Maisy. She loved dancing and I knew that if she wanted a career in dance, London would be the best place to be. My dad never believed that I would leave Tenerife, and even when we actually arrived in the UK, he was still shocked that I had left Tenerife, a now-single mum with three kids and a dog, Lola, who was now 12.

Now that we were here in the UK, the hospitals talked

about ways they could help Maisy more and get her involved with children like her who also had Retinoblastoma. Caroline had been replaced by Gemma as the play specialist and I asked her if there were any children, preferably girls, around Maisy's age who had had Retinoblastoma. I thought it would be nice for her to talk to someone who had been through the same. Unfortunately, she couldn't think of anyone, which was a shame. However, she did mention that Maisy could start attending 'Eye Club' in the school holidays and would let me know when the next date was planned.

Maisy and her brother Harry started school at Squirrels Heath Juniors, not on the first day after the summer holidays like the other children, but a few days later. On their first day I was so nervous, while they were so excited. They couldn't wait to start at their new school. I was especially concerned about Harry as he was worried that his English wasn't good enough. He could speak it, but his writing was not very good. But he ran into school that day, and when I picked him up at the end, I could see he'd had the best day ever.

Maisy enjoyed her day too and managed to make some friends, but she wasn't confident about talking about her eye to anyone that asked. She said she noticed a few girls staring at her, and this continued to happen on a daily basis. She assumed it was because of her eye and in truth she was finding it hard to cope.

One day I collected both kids from school and Maisy looked upset. On the way home I spoke to her, and she said that some kids had been asking about her eye and she didn't know what to say. I asked her if she would feel comfortable taking the album that I made for her to school, to show the children in her class, and then perhaps they would understand more. She agreed so I contacted the school, and they thought it was a great idea.

A few days later she took the album into school, and

when I picked her up, she seemed much brighter. The photo album had been passed around at school and the teacher had read it too. It was even given to other classes in different years. Maisy felt much happier after that, knowing that most of the kids now knew what had happened to her.

I managed to get George into a nursery in the church at Romford Market. I was only offered two half days a week, but it was better than nothing. It felt strange though as George had already been in full-time education doing five full days a week in Tenerife. Unlike Maisy and Harry enjoying their new school, George hated it. He cried every morning and took months to settle, eventually coming to love his nursery, and the teachers.

Having the kids settled helped me feel more settled living back in the UK. I started googling dance schools and found a local school for Maisy to try. In the end, we ended up trying three different dance schools until we found one that suited Maisy - Beverley Marks Stage school. I'd explained to Beverley about Maisy's eye, and Maisy felt comfortable there and made lots of new friends.

Memory from Beverley: *When I first met Maisy she walked into the studio and was immediately uplifted and moved by the music and street dance routine, it was obvious she loved to dance. She was a young child then and mum had explained to us about Maisy's journey and condition, and to be honest we were not expecting the independent, capable little dynamo that was Maisy. She was incredibly easy to teach with her strong focus and listening skills teamed with a natural ability to street dance.*

2ND OCTOBER

It was a lot easier now we were living in England regarding travelling to and from the hospital appointments.

That night, Maisy and I laid on my bed chatting when we both looked at each other; we could hear a clicking noise coming from her new eye. She sat up and it stopped! I told her we'd see how it went, and if it carried on, I'd call the hospital and let them know. After a few days, however, the clicking just stopped on its own. I assumed the new eye just needed time to settle.

I took Maisy to see the dermatologist at Queens's Hospital in Romford. Maisy had to strip to her underwear and lay on the bed while the dermatologist, a lovely lady, slowly checked each of Maisy's moles with a magnifying glass.

There was nothing ominous, but she did come across an interesting mole on Maisy's arm. We'd noticed it, but what we hadn't realised is that up close with the magnifying glass you could clearly see the letter H. It made us laugh as her brother's name is Harry! The dermatologist said she wanted to take photos of it and publish it on to the Internet as it was so interesting. We've since searched but have never found it online.

30ᵀᴴ November

Maisy participated in the East London Street Dance Championships with Beverley Marks Dance School.

Her team, The Freshmans, came first, and Maisy came fifth in her first pair's competition (under 14s category).

41

THE EYE CLUB

2015

*2*nd March 2015
      Another day of waiting but all good news from Mr Hungerford's team at Maisy's cancer check.

A month or so before this day I started to notice that Maisy kept having some kind of tick when she was speaking, but not all the time. She didn't realise she was doing it, but when it started to get worse and more frequent, I started to pull her up on it and ask if she knew about it, but she said she wasn't aware.

The only way I can describe it was that she was pushing her good eye forward like she was trying to stretch it. I was worried about her getting bullied at school as she didn't know she was doing it and therefore couldn't control it.

I mentioned this to Dr Kingston, who confirmed it sounded like a tick, and said she would probably just grow out of it.

Hospital notes: *Mum has noticed that she has started having ticks; mum is going to keep a diary to see if it is related to stress or* *tiredness. Maisy stated that her eye feels dry, for which I have prescribed Systane eye drops.*

30TH MARCH

I'd recently been contacted by the Royal London Hospital asking if we would like free tickets to see a Magic Show at the Mermaid Theatre in London, organised by the Rays of Sunshine charity.

Maisy, Harry, George and I had really good seats in the middle of the theatre. The show involved lots of audience participation and when the comedian threw a toy monkey that landed at Maisy's feet, she was invited onto the stage. She had to sit down at a small desk and pick a card from the magician's hand during a magic trick. She was only on stage a few minutes but loved being part of the show.

Maisy was now doing well at school. All the teachers were kind and really liked her, one even ordered a table magnifying glass to help her with her work. This helped Maisy a lot.

She liked school, but still had the occasional child saying nasty words to her regarding her eye. I'd tell Maisy to just ignore them and explained how bullies target anyone and not to take it personally. But she was older now and more conscious of her looks. She could now see when she needed a new eye. Sometimes the false eye looked more sunken or smaller than her left eye, so this would upset her as she was worried the bullying would become more frequent while she was waiting for a new eye.

In the half-term holidays, we were all invited to 'Eye Club'. We met at the Royal London Hospital where Maisy was greeted by the play specialist, Gemma, and taken to a room with other children who also had Retinoblastoma.

While they played games, the boys and I were invited for tea, coffee and biscuits in the canteen with the other parents. It was nice to have a chat and listen to other families talk about their experiences and the boys were more than happy eating biscuits and colouring.

At lunchtime the play specialist escorted us back to our children to the parents and family room. There were a mixed range of ages, and Maisy told me they had all been playing games and talking about themselves. There was a very young girl maybe about three or four who was constantly taking her eye out and popping it back in as she was so proud of her false eye. Harry and George couldn't stop staring at her as they still hadn't seen Maisy without her eye. The girl's mum kept apologising to everyone. Apparently, she took it out all the time and would run around holding it. It was funny as the little girl really didn't care that everyone was looking at her.

When I had to take Maisy's eye out, we did it in a room at home with just the two of us. I never wanted Maisy to feel uncomfortable, or for the boys to say something that might upset her.

We all ate pizza which was delivered to the room and then took a short train ride with the other families to go bowling, which the boys loved. It was a lovely day out and nice to socialise with other families going through a similar experience to us.

That summer the Eye Club invited us to Clacton-on-Sea for a day, boys included. I drove as it was only an hour away. We all met in a restaurant where we were told the itinerary for the day. We could have full use of all the rides, plus lunch, and free candy and popcorn at the kiosk.

We had great fun going on all the rides. Harry was now nine and George was seven. The four of us went on the 5D ride and chose shooting Zombies as our game. The effects were so good, but within a couple of minutes, George cried and ran out! Maisy and Harry were laughing so much as I ran after him. I had to wait outside with George whilst Maisy and Harry tried all the other 5D games - and why not, it was all paid for!

Lunch was great and the children all had a fab day. We didn't get to speak to many other families as we were all seated on different tables, but there were a few faces I recognised from the hospital appointments.

The Royal London Hospital also gave us tickets to go and see Diversity. They had notes on their system about how Maisy loved dancing and had previously told me that they often get free tickets for concerts and would contact me if something interesting came up. At the time, Maisy loved Diversity, so she was so excited when I told her. We went by train to The SSE Arena Wembley and were shown to a room where we had VIP food and drinks service. Maisy was so happy!

7TH JUNE

Maisy and I got dressed up and went to the Rays of Sunshine Concert at the Royal Albert Hall. Marvin and Rochelle were the presenters, and we were entertained by Pixie Lott, Little Mix and many more. It was a great night and we felt very fortunate to have been gifted free tickets from Gemma, the play specialist.

22ND JUNE

I, along with Maisy, Harry, my sister, Tina and her daughters, Daniella, Isabella and Sienna, all signed up for the 'Race for Life' charity fun run in Basildon. We all brought pink t-shirts to wear apart from Harry who wore his Barcelona football shirt. Race for Life had sent us all pieces of paper to pin on our t-shirts saying who we were running for. Maisy had a picture of herself when she was small on her t-shirt, with the words 'I'm a survivor' printed above. On my piece of paper, I wrote 'I race for life for my daughter Maisy Rose Bradford who beat cancer'. We had loads of fun along the run and raised money for a great cause.

SEPTEMBER 2015

We chose Marshalls Park Academy in Romford for Maisy's senior school as it was a dance academy, and they also had a few children there that were blind or partial sighted. I felt that they had a good team in place to assist with Maisy's needs. We had already met the lovely Mrs McCartney who worked as SENCO (Special Educational Needs Coordinator), and Maisy really liked her.

In the first two years she felt a bit lost. She never had a best mate, and the odd so-called friend would often say something horrible to her about her eye. I had to contact the school a few times regarding certain girls that bullied her. It was a sad time as she was such a lovely girl. But by the time she got to year 10 she had made best friends with four girls - Megan, Amy, Mia and Eloise. Having friendships with these girls definitely gave Maisy more confidence at school.

Maisy really struggled at sports though because she was unable to play certain games as they were considered too dangerous for her, although the school often forgot, and I would have to remind them. When she was made to play, she would then get bullied. For example, she was told to join in a netball game, but she couldn't see the ball, she has a massive blind spot. So, the girls playing were shouting at her to pass the ball or catch it, but Maisy just couldn't see. I had to contact the school and remind them not to put my daughter in that situation again.

I was recommended by the hospital to buy some special sport glasses, which I did in year 9, but they were like swimming goggles. Although she took them to school and told me she wore them, I don't think she ever did. In the end I told the school she wasn't to do sports involving small balls or anything that could harm her. Maisy was upset, but also relieved as she didn't like confrontation and being in an awkward situation, she would just do what she was told by the teachers. I told her many times that she needed to stick up for herself more and to not hold back on saying how she felt. I also reminded her that she needed to be careful to protect her eyes.

42
MORE EYES

2016

1 4th January 2016

Sadly, we had to have our dog, Lola put down. She started having fits in the middle of the night and by the early hours of the morning I knew it was our only option. Maisy came with me to the vets, and I warned her that it would be upsetting seeing the vet put Lola to sleep, but she insisted on coming. Maisy was very brave standing with me watching Lola sleeping, but it was so sad. I still think of her even now. She was the best dog with the kids and we all really miss her.

4TH MARCH

Another new eye fitted at Moorfields eye hospital by Peter.

7TH MARCH

Maisy had an assessment at the Royal London Hospital, where a nurse took her blood pressure and measured her height. She told me that we would be seeing a different paediatrician today as unfortunately Dr Kingston had passed away in January this year. The nurse explained she'd been feeling unwell and died within days. It was really sad to hear this as she truly was a lovely doctor.

Hospital notes: *Maisy has recurrent infections, she is having 1 every month, no headaches, she enjoys attending teenage eye club and continues to spend time dancing. She is now at secondary school which is a dance academy which she enjoys.*

Maisy was still having new eyes made for her every six months as she was growing so much. Even a few months after having a new eye it started looking too small. Peter advised us that this was quite normal and would last until she was around 18, when she'd stop growing. We have quite a collection of different coloured eyes at home, from piercing blue, to dark blue, to green, to hazel coloured; her eye colour changed so much over time, it's so interesting. Every now and then we get all her old false eyes out just to have a look.

We received invitations to attend Rays of Sunshine's, Frankie and Benny's at the SSE Arena, starring Fleur East, Nicole Scherzinger, DNCE, Conor Maynard and many more. Maisy and I had a fabulous night dancing in our chairs and in the aisles.

Rays of Sunshine contacted me and said that Maisy could have another wish; we looked for ages at ideas and searched on the internet at other children's wishes. She still loved dancing, so I came up with the suggestion that she danced on a stage. I mentioned this to the 'make a wish lady' and she said she would have a think.

6TH AUGUST

Maisy called me into her bedroom. She was upset with

her false eye. Already it looked a completely different colour. She looked at herself in the mirror and said, 'I'm ugly'. It broke my heart. I told her she was beautiful and so special, but this continued until it came to the point where Maisy refused to return to school in September with this eye. I contacted Moorfields and explained, but the receptionist said there was a six-month waiting list. I asked her if she would kindly add me to a cancelation list as Maisy was unhappy with her eye and refusing to return to school.

A few days later she called to say there had been a cancelation but with a different oculist. I took the appointment anyway as we were desperate.

She did return to school that September but complained for weeks that her false eye didn't look the same as her good eye.

11ᵀᴴ OCTOBER

A lady called Anne Bradley did the fitting for her new eye at Moorfields this time and told us she would be in touch when the eye was ready. We were a little bit gutted that we were unable to see Peter, but Anne said he was really busy, and Maisy desperately needed a new eye as soon as possible.

26ᵀᴴ OCTOBER

Anne was nice, and thankfully the eye looked good, so Maisy was happy. That same day I received a phone call from Maisy's school, from Mrs McCartney the SENCO. She said that a new student had started who had also retinoblastoma as a baby, and now had a false eye.

The young girl was a year older than Maisy and Mrs McCartney asked me if I would kindly speak to her mum. She said that her false eye was nowhere near as good as

Maisy's and the young girl was really struggling with her confidence. I agreed to talk to the mum and awaited her phone call.

The next day the mum called me. She was Polish, and her daughter's name was Claudia. We had a quick chat and arranged to meet for a coffee. She only lived ten minutes away from me, so we met in Romford. We got on well and I explained about Maisy and the hospitals where she was treated. She was so grateful for my help. Claudia had not had a new eye false for years and her local GP was not helping her. She said Claudia hated her appearance because of this. I wrote down the hospital numbers and the prosthetics department and explained that she needed to see her local GP and ask to be referred to Moorfields.

A few months later, I got a phone call from the mum who said that she'd done what I had advised and now Claudia had a new eye and was so happy. I was just grateful that I could help her.

43

THRILLER

2017

*W*e received a letter from Make a Wish addressed to Maisy - an invitation to rehearse with the cast of *Thriller*! There was also a cheque for Maisy to buy a new outfit especially for the occasion. We would all be getting picked up and driven to London. It was all very exciting!!

17ᵀᴴ JANUARY 2017

Make a Wish said that we'd be picked up at 1pm. Maisy, Harry, George and I all got ready and kept looking out of the window hoping it was going to be a limo that was collecting us. We lived down a small dead-end road in Romford and I worried that if it was a limo the driver might have trouble driving down our road.

Suddenly the boys saw it! 'It's a limo!' they shouted. A big white limo was driving slowly down the road. We all raced outside, and the driver greeted us and opened the door. Inside was a bottle of champagne for me, and fizzy drinks for the kids.

The journey was great. The kids loved that they could see out of the windows, but no one could see in. People were staring at us, and the kids felt so special. At the theatre on Shaftesbury Avenue, we were met by a lady who worked for Make a Wish. We followed her to a side entrance and were shown to a small room. The lady gave Maisy, Harry and George a Thriller programme each, then gave us a tour of the theatre and backstage.

When we were backstage, we could see the Thriller costumes hanging up and a photographer took some fab photos of us trying on some of the masks. Maisy found Michael Jackson's hat, so she tried it on and posed for a photo. We also saw where the cast have their hair and make-up done. As we were walking around, some of the performers started to arrive through the backstage entrance. They were all young and all said hello to us.

We were then taken onto the stage where the lady explained to Maisy, Harry and George about the lights and how the curtains worked. She then told me and the boys to take a seat anywhere in the auditorium, which was empty at the time, so we sat three rows from the front.

Maisy stayed on-stage, and by this time a few of the cast members had appeared too. Maisy was shy at first when the cast started chatting to her, then 'Michael Jackson' came over and started asking her questions. He shouted to the rest of the cast, 'Maisy is a dancer you know!' The cast were smiling and one of the girls asked her if she wanted to join in their warm-up.

The music was loud, and the cast started their warm-up with Maisy copying them from behind. It was so lovely and emotional to see her up there dancing with the cast. One of the young fellas then asked Maisy to dance for them. She wasn't at all shy now so was more than happy to perform. The cast made a circle around her as Fleur East's Play that

Sax boomed throughout the theatre. Maisy was showing off her dance moves and giving it 100 per cent while the cast cheered her on. She was loving it, and at the end they joined in with her dancing, doing their own thing. The cast were going crazy, cheering and high fiving each other and Maisy when the song had finished. She was so happy and pleased with herself. The cast then asked her for her Thriller programme, and they all took it in turns to sign their autographs next to their photos.

Afterwards we were taken back outside as the cast needed to get ready to perform for the evening's show. We were shown outside to the street for us to wait until the theatre doors were open. As we walked out, I heard my name called. My sister, Tina, her husband, Kevin, and my two nieces, Isabella and Sienna had booked tickets to come and see the show!

My sister was seated quite far from us so we said we would see them in the interval. We took our seats, which unfortunately were very far back on the ground level, and Maisy was unable to see much! I didn't want to complain, but I had to at least ask if there were any seats closer. I left the kids there while I walked to the box office to ask the lady, but she was unable to help but said to ask again at the interval.

So, for the first half we stayed seated where we were and sadly Maisy couldn't see most of the show. She still enjoyed it, and in the interval, we were given seats on the first deck to the left side of the stage. She still struggled to see that far but the seats were much better, and the show was brilliant; we all really enjoyed it.

After the show we said goodbye to my sister and her family as we had dinner booked across the road at the Rainforest Café. It was our first visit to this restaurant and the kids loved the décor, the boys especially. We chatted about our day whilst we enjoyed a lovely dinner in tropical surroundings.

When we were ready to leave, we could see our driver waiting for us outside the theatre still – he'd been waiting there all day! We had a lovely drive home looking at London and all the lights; it really was a great experience, and not just for Maisy but for the boys too.

Tina's memory: *We loved watching Thriller that night and Maisy had had the best day.*

44

PUPILS IN THE POST

4 th June 2017

Maisy, the boys and I were on our way to Moorfields in London as Maisy was getting a new eye fitted. We sat outside in a small waiting room with walls decorated in Minions pictures, so we all had silly photos taken, Harry included. After the appointment we went for lunch and a walk around Covent Garden.

11TH OCTOBER

Hospital notes: *Maisy's mum has called to say that her eye keeps falling out, mainly falls out when she is lying down.*

I remember the first time this happened. I was sitting on the bed chatting with Maisy. She was lying down, and her eye just popped out. We laughed and wondered how it had happened. We put it back in and said we hoped it didn't fall out like that in public. I said to her if the eye was to ever fall out, she should cover her eye with one hand and grab her false eye before anyone stepped on it.

Sometimes when Maisy has had an eye infection, she's had to go to school wearing a big eye plaster, which she hated. Although it didn't affect her sight as she couldn't see from that side anyway, she'd get bullied just for wearing the plaster. She would come home and beg me to put her eye back in for school the following day. Sometimes the infection was still in her eye socket, but she refused to go to school without her eye in. So, I would put it back in and hope that it wasn't too uncomfortable for her and that it didn't fall out at school. Luckily for her it never did.

24TH OCTOBER

We had been given tickets to see Fleur East at the O2 Arena, from Gemma at the Royal London Hospital, who had been given them from Rays of Sunshine. It was a great evening and we had good seats. Maisy loved music and was happy sitting in her chair dancing and singing. Fleur East's performance was amazing, and Maisy was a huge fan at the time.

6TH MARCH 2017

> **Hospital notes:** *Maisy complains of discharge from right socket, status is stable, and chloramphenicol prescribed. Tumours stable and she looks healthy, and her false eye looks good.*

11TH APRIL

Fitting and painting done for her new eye.

Hospital notes: *Maisy's eye has been popping out when lying down.*

9TH MAY

At this appointment Anne said that she would send the eye by post as she was sure that the new one would be fine, and it would save us a journey. Maisy and I laughed at the fact that she would receive a new eye in the post. Not many people can say that they had an eye sent in the post!

18TH MAY

I waited until she got home from school. It was strange to see her opening her package to discover it was her new eye. We popped it straight in and the fit looked perfect.

21ST MAY

Lucie, my cousin, her daughter Millie and I signed ourselves up for the Mud Run at Basildon for Race for Life again. We'd been sent a big sticker to write who we were running for and then to stick it to our t-shirt. I had a pink t-shirt with a lovely photo of Maisy printed on the back, and above in big letters, My Survivor. On my front sticker it said, 'I race for Life for… Nanny Rene, Joni Mai Stevens, ANGELS IN THE SKY.'

OCTOBER 2017

Maisy travelled to Paris to perform at the 'International Festival of Dance and Performing Arts' with Beverly Marks stage school. The judges were from Disney Performing Arts.

She had the best time learning routines and dancing in the parade. I was so proud of her wanting to go and then being chosen to perform. This was a great experience for her and one she'll never forget.

8TH DECEMBER 2017

Hospital notes: *Painting done for new eye, grandma with her today, procedure explained, Maisy well, top lid tilted tried to change this without occurring pressure on lower lid.*

45

A MATTER OF COLOUR

2018

*3*rd January 2018

Hospital notes: *Artificial eye, iris too green, needs more grey, Anne.*

22ND JANUARY

I was disappointed the colour didn't look the same as her good eye. Maisy noticed it too when she was looking in the mirror, but I could see straight away that the eye colour could be better. I told Anne the colour didn't look the same and she said she'd make it greener. We left the hospital with the same eye she arrived in. Maisy was upset as the eye she had was too small and she knew she would have to wait weeks for her new eye.

28TH JANUARY

I had contacted the hospital and politely complained that

the last two eyes Anne had made for Maisy were not the same colour as her good eye. I asked if we could have Peter again as his eyes were so good and it was horrible hearing Maisy get upset about having to walk around with two completely different coloured eyes!

17TH FEBRUARY

We were so pleased to see Peter and the new eye he had made for Maisy at Moorfields Eye Hospital. We didn't mention Anne, but I said that we were happy to have him again. Maisy was much happier too, and the eye he had made was perfect.

19TH MARCH

We received a letter from the Learning Assessment Centre stating that Maisy is a happy and very active child. They also had carried out a visual assessment due to Maisy getting headaches:

When Maisy wears glasses she can see six metres in front of her, while the fully sighted see 30 metres. Maisy needs to continue to sit at the front in all classes. Maisy will need enlarged examination papers; she cannot see faint images. When approaching Maisy from behind, try to approach her from the left side.
Try to maintain eye-to-eye contact with Maisy's left eye
Avoid unnecessary hazards, obstacles, half-open doors, windows.
Maisy should never be expected to share a work sheet or textbook.
Check that she is in the best position to see demonstrations.
A copy of this letter was also sent to her school.

It made me sad reading this. Maisy is so happy most of the time she just gets on with life and sometimes we forget that she is partially sighted. But when you get letters like this, it reminds you of the struggles that she does have and will always have.

5TH APRIL

The Champions of Magic Show was in the same location as before at The Mermaid Theatre in Puddle Dock and I'd been gifted six tickets by Rays of Sunshine. Maisy, George, Harry and I met our cousins, Lucie and Max, near the theatre. Max really loved magic at the time, so he was very excited.

We were greeted by the Rays of Sunshine team and had our photos taken and then shown to our seats. We were at the right side of the stage near the front. The show was just as good as the first time we saw it. The audience were involved in playing games and the kids really enjoyed the show, Max especially.

5TH JUNE

We had a low vision check and a cancer check-up at Bart's. We saw Zishan Naeem who was always great with Maisy, asking her about school and what she had been doing. She had the eye test and again struggled to see certain letters, letters that I found so easy to read. I sat there quietly whilst he carried out his tests, but I felt upset that she couldn't see the easiest of letters. However, he said that her vision hadn't deteriorated so that was good news.

From a young age doctors advised that glasses would not help Maisy's vision, but she was getting frequent headaches. Dr Zishan tried a few magnifying glasses and found that this helped Maisy, so we were able to take a few home. He also advised me to take her for an eye test at our local optician.

Her cancer check that day went well; she was always so brave sitting there in the chair. This time she was confident enough to remove her eye herself. I was proud of her as she'd never done it before in these checks. The doctor was happy with the stable tumours, and happy with her false eye.

28ᵀᴴ JUNE

Notes from Peter: *Replicated previous shape and patient very happy with comfort and made slightly wider to stretch socket.*

He took Maisy's eye out with his fingers. I've never tried it this way as I always use a sucker. He mixed up the custard as we've always called it, and then placed the funnel in the eye and filled the funnel with the yellow liquid. Maisy said it felt cold. It must feel so strange. Within a couple of minutes, it set hard, and he took the mould out. He then took measurements of where the pupil should be on the moulding and captured photos of Maisy's eye for the colour match. He then left the room and took Maisy's old false eye to give it a good clean. As soon as he returned, he popped her eye back in and we were done.

10ᵀᴴ JULY

I'd made an appointment at Specsavers in Hornchurch and explained to the optician about Maisy's sight. We were surprised when the lady advised us that glasses would help Maisy for reading and looking at the white board. At the time glasses were fashionable for teenagers so she was more than happy to wear them. She tried out a few pairs and chose some black geeky ones and some clear coloured glasses too. They suited her and she liked them, so she was happy to wear them around the house and at school.

It didn't last long, maybe a few months, and then she stopped wearing them. As for the magnifying glasses, they never left her bedroom because she was too embarrassed to use them at school in case she got bullied. So instead, she carried on struggling at school.

46
THE LETTER

This letter made me very sad, and I did have a cry after reading it. It took me two days to process everything until I felt ready to speak to Maisy about it without getting upset in front of her. It read;

Maisy was last seen in the hospital department on 5th June 2018 where she was accompanied by her mother. Her remaining left eye has a large tumour in the central part of the retina. This part of the retina allows for clarity of vision: hence why the vision is below satisfactory in the remaining left eye. Maisy also has a visual field defect whereby she has an area in her central field of view that she cannot see, and as a result this means that she will unfortunately be unable to drive in the future.

That's what made me cry... most 17-year-olds can't wait to start learning to drive, and this had been taken away from her! It really upset me for a couple of days while I was trying to find the courage to tell Maisy.

The letter continued;

The visual acuity is at a significantly reduced level, especially for her age. Maisy achieved this acuity by using eccentric fixation, whereby she used head movements on and off centre with her eye and view the letters on the screen using her peripheral (outer) vision. A letter that a child with normal vision would see at 6 metres cannot be seen by Maisy unless it is made at least five times bigger in size. At near she is able to see a print with a font size N10 from approximately 20cm away. This suggests that she will benefit from larger print when reading. Magnifiers will be particularly useful in allowing Maisy to read more easily and with less strain on the eye. She would need to position books and objects in such a way that she can maximise the use of vision (place things in the left side) As a result of having monocular vision (using vision from one eye) Maisy will not appreciate depth perception in the same ways as someone using both or their eyes together. We all need two eyes working together to truly appreciate 3-D/stereoscopic vision. Children with monocular vision may struggle to appreciate depth perception, and certain tasks like judging speed of moving things, and navigating around different levels like steps and stairs may be problematic. Children may be seen to bump into things more often, and busy environments like the corridor/hallways may take longer to navigate around. Some children can find busy environments frightening and daunting as there is too much information to try and take in. Maisy should be encouraged to use which ever head movement she feels necessary in order to view her surrounds/any objects which she wishes to view. She may also be seen to hold objects very closely and this too should not be discouraged. It is useful in Maisy's case for teachers and peers to approach her from the left side and for activities to take place on her left side; otherwise, she will be required to turn her head more in order to use her vision.

Maisy's vision is further complicated by the presence of nystagmus: this is where the eye constantly wobbles.

Reading this made me realise everything that she's had to deal with and will have to deal with in her future. I sometimes take her for granted as she's so confident most of the time and generally just gets on with it.

I didn't want to speak to anyone about this letter. I kept it to myself to try and process it and work out how I was going to tell Maisy. I remember calling my sister a few days later to talk about it; she too agreed it was such a shame.

A few days later I sat Maisy down and I read her the letter. I could see her getting upset, so I quickly changed the bad news into a positive to try and make her feel better.

I said cars are a pain and costly, and you can rely on friends and family to pick you up, plus when you're out drinking with friends you can drink and won't be the designated driver. She had a little smile, but I knew deep down she was sad, and we continued to speak about this over the next few days.

I guess eventually she got her head around it and accepted it, but it was a real shame for her, and I totally understood how she was annoyed that she couldn't even try to drive. But that was that, the chance to drive had been taken away from her.

Now when we go camping on a big field, I let her drive the car. To be perfectly honest, she isn't very good at it so it's probably a blessing! But at least she can have fun trying, and hopefully she doesn't feel quite so left out when her friends are talking about driving.

47

DAYS GOING OUT, AND NEW EYES GOING IN

DANCING

1 5th August 2018
A new eye.

19TH AUGUST

Gemma, the hospital play specialist had arranged a day out at Clacton Pier. The kids had loved it last time we went with the team. We had to meet at 10am where we checked in, met the play specialists and had a drink. Then we had to choose what we'd all like for lunch. We were then told the itinerary of the day, but basically, we had a pass for the rides and could go to the kiosks for candyfloss, and it was all paid for. We all had a great morning on the rides and then we met back up with the rest of the families for lunch.

1ST MARCH 2019

Another new eye, and another added to her collection.

. . .

4TH MARCH

The lady at the low vision clinic was really chatty and good with Maisy. The vision test again made me realise what little she can see from far away. Some letters she really battled with. Because Maisy gets on with life so well and never complains, it was sad to sit there and listen to her struggle.

Even though we were always told that glasses would never help Maisy, I explained that the local optician had said that glasses would help her. Maisy had her glasses on her, so the lady made her wear them and take more tests. She could see that with the prescription lenses she was using, they did help her.

The lady gave me a new glasses prescription and advised me to take this to the local optician to get a new pair. The problem was that Maisy no longer liked wearing them, they were no longer fashionable. In the end she refused outright to wear them, so we never bothered going back to Specsavers.

14TH JULY

Maisy was asked to dance at Brands Hatch with her school, Marshalls Park Academy.

I had to pay for the extra dance classes to learn the new routine, and for the t-shirt that she had to wear on the day. But I was so happy for her; what an experience this was going to be.

When the day arrived, I had to drop Maisy off at school early on a Saturday morning to meet the teachers and the coach. I had thought about going to watch her and, looking back, I wished I had. My brother, Gary, and his girlfriend, Lena, and son, Joe, had already arranged to go that weekend, plus my mum and dad would be there for the day too. So, she had them all there to watch her.

They managed to watch it on the big screens but weren't sure if they actually saw Maisy or not as all the girls looked the same in their t-shirts. My brother sent me a video of the dance from the screen that he managed to record. There were so many dancing on the track that it was very hard to spot her.

I watched the clip of all the children dancing though and was so proud. Anytime I watch her dance I get teary eyed, even now. She had the best day being on the track and seeing Lewis Hamilton. We sat together that night and watched the recording and she showed me where she was on the track. She appeared for all of two seconds!

4ᵀᴴ Sᴇᴘᴛ

> **Hospital notes:** *Maisy is concerned about sitting her GCSE exams, she does not feel that SENCO are helping her enough and sometimes when she arrives in classes, teachers have forgotten her and not prepared her work to be enlarged and she is not confident to ask the teacher so will the spend the time in the class struggling. We contacted the school to explain further help is needed for Maisy.*

Mrs McCartney her SENCO teacher is lovely and really likes Maisy, but like me, she sometimes forgets she needs help because she just gets on with it. We told Maisy she needs to tell the teachers and not to struggle through everything.

Also, we received a letter from the local GP stating that Maisy had been to visit due to her feeling dizzy and faint on a few occasions. I remember this happening where she would be fine one minute, then the next would start to feel dizzy and turn pale. I'd give her a drink of water and tell her to sit until it passed. This happened on more than a few occasions, but the doctors checked her, and everything showed as normal. I bought Maisy some vitamins to help her boost her energy, which seemed to work as these episodes gradually stopped.

7ᵀᴴ OCTOBER
    Eye fitting

3ᴿᴰ DECEMBER
    Maisy had a new eye fitted at Moorfields Eye Hospital by Peter, it looked so good, and the colour was perfect.

48

A NEW DECADE

2020

2   1ˢᵗ January 2020
       Maisy performed with Beverley Marks Stage
School in an amazing show called POWER at the Queens's
Theatre. She'd performed many times there before with the
school. They were all fantastic shows, and we always
purchased the DVD so we could keep it to look back on.

12ᵀᴴ FEBRUARY

I was sat in the audience waiting for Maisy's GCSE dance
performance at her school, the Marshalls Park Academy. The
show began with lots of her friends and classmates all
performing and then Maisy came on stage. Her name was in
big letters on the screen, and she danced beautifully to a song
called *Don't Get Me Wrong* by Lewis Capaldi. It was amazing. I
got teary-eyed and she achieved an A in dance GCSE - no
surprise really as she is a brilliant dancer.

14ᵀᴴ FEBRUARY

When she first came home with the letter announcing a school skiing trip to Austria, I wasn't sure if this would be a good idea for Maisy. I contacted the school to speak to Miss McCartney, the SENCO teacher, and asked for more details. Maisy is such a clumsy person, and I was worried that firstly she may hurt herself, and secondly, that with her poor eyesight she might get lost. The school assured me there were many teachers attending so that put my mind at rest... a little. So, Sam and I paid for her trip and brought the relevant clothing needed.

I'm so pleased we let her go. Her group did a challenge; fastest person to get down the slope, and Maisy won! She got a certificate and was also crowned 'best skier'. Who'd have thought it, our clumsy Maisy! She came back with loads of stories to tell and made lots of new friends.

28TH FEBRUARY

Great Ormond Street for a yearly check-up for any lumps or pains.

> **Hospital Notes:** *Maisy doing very well, and they have no concerns regarding her general health. She has no history of headaches nor any abnormal soft tissue or bony masses. She has multiple naevi (skin marks) but one in particular on her low to mid back, her mum is concerned about this as it appears to have changed in appearance and is slightly raised. I will refer her. She is aware of risks of secondary cancers and to avoid smoking.*

I advised the hospital that we had recently spoken to a local GP via video call and he looked at the moles that we were concerned about, and we were waiting to be referred.

I phoned the doctors to chase this, and the consultant also wrote to my local GP asking them to refer her. She was eventually referred to Queen's hospital in Romford to be checked again in person where it was agreed that it would be better to have the moles removed.

27ᵀᴴ MARCH

Covid had arrived and we were reduced to video call appointments, the first to a lovely consultant called Dr Catriona Duncan. This call was to explain to Maisy how the effects of her cancer may affect the future. It was a conversation that we'd never really had. I knew there could be a problem with Maisy trying to start a family, but I never worried about it so much then as it was a long way off. The doctor explained to Maisy why she developed RB and the three implications that would affect her. We also received this in writing:

1. The altered RB gene caused you to develop Retinoblastoma; you are now too old to get another retinoblastoma.
2. There is a small chance that you could get another tumour related to the RB gene. Most people do not get these other tumours. When they occur, they can affect any part of the body and tend to grow in bones, muscle or skin. The tumours in bones or muscle tend to show as lumps or pains that you cannot explain that do not get better over a couple of weeks. The skin tumours are melanomas which are 'nasty moles.' If you get anything that you are worried about, you should always go to your GP first.
3. When you have children there will be a 50- 50 chance that you would pass on the altered retinoblastoma gene to a child and a 50-50 chance

that you would pass on the normal RB gene to a child. A child who inherits the normal copy of the gene will have no increase chance of developing RB and would not pass the condition to their future children.

- A child that inherits that altered gene would be very likely to get RB. Most people say that they would want to arrange genetic testing on a baby when it's born so that it can start having regular eye checks from early in life if these are needed.
- Some people feel that they would not want to have a child who might get RB and there are tests that we can do around a pregnancy to help with this.

Maisy was only 16 years old, so this was not something she was thinking about currently, but it was still sad to hear that she will have to go through the worry when she does decide to have a baby. However, we will cross that road together when it comes to it.

AND JUST LIKE THAT, Maisy had left school. She did well in her GCSE exams and was happy but all she ever wanted was to be a dancer so we visited dance schools to apply for the next step. She really loved Urdang in London, as she attended the summer school there and really enjoyed it, and she also liked Italia Conti. Sadly though, she wasn't accepted into either of those colleges, so she applied to a local college and was accepted to study dance at Dimensions in South Essex College.

Her plan was to study for a year and then re-apply at Urdang for the course she really wanted. She also looked at other courses as she wasn't happy that she didn't get accepted at Urdang and considered that maybe she could study something completely different and then return to dance.

Maisy was also interested in criminology and forensics, as well as personal training. She visited the open evening for both courses and when she came home, she told me all about it. The forensics course sounded really interesting.

But over the next few weeks she kept waking up in the night and getting upset, worrying about the dance course she'd chosen. We both sat and talked about the courses and the benefits, and although she still wanted to do dance, she only wanted to study it if it was at the Urdang Academy. She decided she didn't want to do the Dimensions dance course after all, so she applied for, and was accepted on, the forensics and criminology course.

5TH AUGUST

Maisy and I sat in a small room in the Royal London Hospital waiting for her to have her two moles removed. We both had to wear our masks due to covid. The nurse visited and checked Maisy's height and weight, had a chat and then said she would be returning soon with numbing cream. Maisy wasn't nervous at all; she even did a TikTok in the waiting room!

The nurse returned and rubbed the cream on Maisy's back and told us that she would have to go in the room on her own, but Maisy was fine with this. The nurse was lovely and chatty, and made Maisy feel comfortable. The nurse told her to take her phone in so she could play games to distract herself.

I sat waiting and hoping that she was okay, as I knew she wasn't great with pain. I messaged to see if she was on her phone, but she didn't reply. Then, after about thirty minutes, then she walked back into the waiting room smiling and said it wasn't too painful. When she lifted her top to show me, I was shocked at how big the incisions were and was upset that she had to go through that and have more scars. She seemed okay though, and said the nurse chatted to her the whole time she was in the room, so that helped.

She had to stay seated for 20 minutes until the nurse knew that Maisy was okay and didn't feel dizzy or sick. She was fine and we were able to leave, and the nurse said that they'd be in touch if they found any problems with the removed moles.

Over the next couple of days, we had to keep the areas dry and make sure they were clean, so we kept changing the dressing and Maisy seemed fine.

However, three days after she'd had the moles removed, we were driving to York to visit my parents for the weekend when Maisy said her back was sore. Not long after we arrived in York Maisy started to feel sick and dizzy and her face went so white. I thought the stitches might have become infected but when I checked, I noticed that some of the bottom stitches had come out, and the area was inflamed and open. I phoned 111 and after about an hour a doctor called. I explained what Maisy had been through at the hospital and told him I was worried as the scarring had a small gap. He didn't seem concerned but explained that unfortunately the scarring would now be bigger. I felt terrible that she had gone through this and now she will be left with a bigger, redder scar then she should have.

I drove to Tesco's pharmacy with my mum to collect antibiotics and left Maisy with my dad and the boys. As soon as I returned, I gave Maisy the medication and she spent the night lying on the sofa.

The next morning Maisy said she felt better even though I was up with her in the night as she was being sick. She still looked pale, and as the day went on, she wasn't improving and was now in pain with her lower back where the mole had been removed.

I phoned 111 again and once more explained to the doctor how Maisy was feeling. This time he suggested that Maisy could be allergic to penicillin. I drove again to Tesco's to collect different antibiotics and the next day she felt much better.

When the moles finally healed, I brought bio-oil for her to keep rubbing on the areas to help with the scarring. I constantly put cream on the scars to help them heal but they're still quite big and red. Luckily for Maisy they're on her back so she can't see them.

27ᵀᴴ SEPTEMBER

We'd kindly been given tickets to Alton Towers by Gemma at the Royal London hospital. The sun was shining, and we had a great day with VIP treatment, going on as many rides as we could. It was a day of family fun with lots of laughter, just what we needed.

49
WHEN STUDENT BECOMES
TEACHER

*O*ctober 2020
Maisy had been helping her dance teacher, Sam Fleet, in his class with the younger children, which she loved. She was then happy to be asked by Beverley to teach them on a Wednesday night.

On her very first class she was nervous when I dropped her off, but when I collected her, she came out buzzing. She loved it. She still teaches the Wednesday class occasionally, and still loves it.

Notes that Beverly **Fleet wrote about Maisy:** *Through hard work, independence and dedication Maisy has become the dancer she is today and is a credit to our school and her mum. It has been very warming and satisfying to see her progress and teaching at our school. When I think of Maisy, she has my respect as 'Maisy the dancer' who deals with things herself, and I am proud to be her principal.*

. . .

NOTES FROM SAM FLEET, Maisy's street dance teacher: *Maisy has been a huge inspiration to teach. She is one of the most committed students I've ever taught. She loves to dance, it's her passion. She is a good role model for the younger students. Her story is beyond inspiring, she comes with humility and gratitude to every class. She is a leading example in every rehearsal, and what she has been through is an inspiring story for all of us to stay encouraged and uplifted.*

3ʳᵈ November

We never have to wait long to see for an eye fitting with Peter, and he always greets us with a smile. He's so good with Maisy, asking her about college and what she's been up to! We were in there less than an hour then we walked to Pret-a-Manger for some yummy lunch, one of mine and Maisy's favourite food places, and still is. Maisy particularly loves the cauliflower and kale macaroni cheese.

16ᵀᴴ DECEMBER

We were only at Moorfields about 30 minutes. Once fitted, the new eye looked great, and Maisy said it felt comfortable.

50

MOTHER'S PRIDE

2021

*T*he first time Maisy took her eye out by herself and completely on her own was recently at the age of 17. She had an infection and didn't ask me, just did it herself. She's now able to take it out and put it back in without any guidance or need for me to be there. The false eyes now are so much better. Each eye that she's had made improves every time.

17ᵗʰ July 2021

Maisy was teaching at Beverley Marks Dance School and asked me to come and watch. I was Maisy's driver on Saturdays dropping her off and picking her up. Today she wasn't dancing only teaching, so I sat outside the hall watching through the window. It was emotional seeing her so confident and bossy, but really good with the young girls. She was teaching them a dance to a new Little Mix song, Confetti. I remember as we left, after she'd said goodbye to her students, I gave her a squeeze and told her how proud I am of her.

. . .

GOING through this horrible experience with Maisy has made me a stronger person but I feel I lack sympathy sometimes. I remember when Maisy was going through all the above - the operations, the side effects, the blood transfusions - and then when people around me would say that they were suffering with colds or flu, the voice inside my head would be saying 'try having cancer and go through what we have all just been through, then moan about it. Think yourself bloody lucky!'

However, would Maisy be the person she is now if she hadn't gone through all of this? Luckily for her she was so young and doesn't remember any of it. For the rest of my family and close friends we will remember everything like it was yesterday. I still get upset talking about some of what she went through, and I have to admit that writing this book was extremely hard. But I wanted to write it not just for Maisy. Yes, I want her to know all the details of what she's been through and to know what a little fighter she was. But I also wanted to write it for families like us that may be going through the same, or something similar. There is hope, something we didn't have at the start, but Maisy is still here, and she's amazing.

'Amazing Maisy' is what Tina calls her, and she is. For any child to have to go through this ordeal and to come out the other side of it fit, well and healthy, is just incredible. If it gives just one family a little hope that their child has a good fighting chance to be okay, then that's why I spent many hours putting my words to screen.

I'm so glad I had kept an album full of notes, photos and hospital letters, or I wouldn't have been able to write this book. Whilst writing it, many memories came back to me that I'd forgotten about, and I also learnt new stories from family members that I don't recollect.

The more time I spent writing this book, the more it made me realise that this book would be good for Maisy to read now she's an adult, for her to look back at what she went through at such a tiny age, at what she survived, and to see what an amazing young woman she is.

On her 18ᵗʰ birthday we had the best celebration. She so deserved it, and we had the best day and night, and she looked so beautiful in her emerald-green dress.

The day after her birthday she had a tattoo booked in at Savannah Ink in Hornchurch, for which she was excited, but nervous too. We'd been thinking of a great first tattoo for Maisy prior to her 18th and Maisy decided that she wanted to have a tattoo of an eye to represent her false eye.

We looked at many ideas of eye tattoos on Pinterest and found a few ideas that we sent to Conor the tattoo artist. I gave Maisy the idea to maybe have a quote written underneath the eye, but again it took us a while to find exactly the right quote that was perfect for Maisy.

I sat with her for the first hour and half, and I can honestly say she didn't even flinch. I was really surprised at this as normally she's not very good with pain. So, I left Maisy with Conor and went back to work, excited to see the finished result.

When she arrived home, she had a huge smile on her face and said she was so happy with it. It really was amazing, and the details were so good. Conor had done such a good job. I felt emotional looking at it as it was so special to her.

But I also told her 'No more tattoos!' But do they listen? She's since had a flower tattooed on her inner arm.

I've always made her believe she can do anything; she just has to try. Of course, I wished this had never happened to Maisy, but she's here and loves life. This cancer hasn't stopped her. She has a great social life, a good group of friends, and a family that adore her.

I hope that any other families currently on a similar journey will be able to stay positive, keep smiling and be strong.

The End

EPILOGUE

$\mathcal{T}$o bring you up to date as I write this in August 2023, Maisy has since completed two years at Southend College with really great results in Forensics and Criminology.

However, to become a crime detective she needed two years' work experience within the police force, so she was looking for opportunities online every day, but with no luck. All the police vacancies required full vision.

I spoke to a friend, Jo, who works in the police force, and she gave me the contact number for someone Maisy could speak to. Maisy contacted the person and explained that she would do any job in the police, she just wanted someone to give her a chance. We even found a link for people with disabilities who were looking to work within the force, but there were never any jobs.

Weeks went by with still no luck. Maisy was beginning to feel very low about herself and was frustrated that the college had not informed her of this before she wasted two years studying.

I sat with Maisy and suggested she thought about a

different career, but she had no idea what else she wanted to do and was not willing to return to college. She was now applying for any jobs just so she could get some experience, bar work, shop work, cafes or sales. Of the 50-plus jobs she applied for, only two replied. One was for a job in a local pub and one for a sales team in London, and she went to both interviews. At the pub, Maisy said the staff were lovely and the lady who interviewed her really liked her, so she really thought she had a good chance of getting the job. But then she never heard any more. The sales job in London involved working with lots of people her own age but she said she didn't think she could be a saleswoman. However, they really liked her and offered her the job. She didn't take it, but at least it made her feel a bit more positive about herself.

She was now spending all day in her room, still applying for jobs and still feeling low. She'd also visited the job centre in hope they had contacts within the police, but they couldn't help her either.

Finally, she received a reply from an agency they were looking for SEN (Special Educational Needs) teachers for a local disability school. The job sounded really good and rewarding, and Maisy thought that this maybe something that she could see herself doing. She had the interview over the phone and the lady asked her to complete an application and told her that she'd be in touch. She never heard from the agency again.

She attended another appointment at the job centre and was advised to delete the information on her CV about being partially sighted. Over the next few days, she applied for even more jobs and received a lot more replies, which then annoyed her even more, as she felt she'd been discriminated against for being partially sighted. One of the replies was from another agency looking for an SEN teacher's assistant, similar to the job she was interested in before.

She went to the interview at the school in Upminster and phoned me on her way home. She'd got the job!

She was very nervous and anxious on her first day and messaged me on her lunch break to say all the other teachers were so nice and she was loving the job.

She continued doing well in the role and really bonded with the kids. However, most days she would come home exhausted, sometimes upset if she'd had a bad day with a child, but the job was also very rewarding.

She'd been working there a few weeks and still no one knew about her eye. Maisy and I had spoken a few times about her work colleagues not knowing, but she said she felt awkward starting the conversation, and none of the other teachers had asked her about it. Even so, she was still worrying about what they would say when they found out.

Karen Reynolds was another teacher's assistant at the school who Maisy got on really well with her from day one. Maisy calls her, her work mum.

Memory from Karen: *I met Maisy on her first day working at the school in Upminster and took her under my wing as she reminded me of my own daughter.*

After several weeks of working with Maisy, we were sitting eating lunch and talking about disabilities within the children in our class. Maisy told me she had cancer when she was a baby and lost her eye. I was so shocked and amazed that this young girl had confided in me. I told her I noticed her eye but assumed she had a lazy eye. Maisy was very open to answering all my questions as I was just so shocked. She was so calm about it all.

That day Maisy came home with a big smile on her face and explained that everyone at school knew about her sight, and she was relieved they now knew the truth.

Maisy is still enjoying her job and is really good in dealing with disruptive behaviour, which is why, from September when school returns, Maisy will be moved into a slightly more challenging class.

At the time of writing this, she is currently travelling around Thailand with her cousin Isabella, having the time of her life. Perks of having the summer holidays off. As her mum, I have no hesitation in saying she should make the most of every fun moment that comes in life. She absolutely deserves it.

ACKNOWLEDGMENTS

Thank you to my lovely family who helped and supported me through Maisy's treatment. Without them I would not be the strong woman I am today.